MASTER PIECES

RICHARD HELLER

Master Pieces

OVAL PUBLISHING
1996

First published in 1996 by
Oval Publishing
30 Crewdson Road
London SW9 0LJ

A catalogue record for this book is available from
the British Library

Typeset in New Century 10/12pt by
Scriptmate Editions
Manufacture coordinated in UK by
Book-in-Hand Ltd 20 Shepherds Hill, London N6 5AH

Preface

"EACH week in The Mail On Sunday RICHARD HELLER gives a dazzling, original, and brilliantly funny insight into the secret stories which shape the world we live in. RICHARD HELLER's logic defies gravity and answers only to the law of levity, like the bubbles in a glass of champagne. Blending sparky one-liners and gorgeous cadences into an exotic cocktail of laughter, RICHARD HELLER truly deserves his title of MASTER PIECES — he raises the standard of comic writing to heights never before attempted, let alone achieved..."

Er, thank you. Most gratifying. An excellent piece of hype.

It shows once again: if you want a job done properly, do it yourself...

But seriously. In The Mail On Sunday I do try to spotlight stories which deserve to be better known and then find the funny side of them. Master Pieces is a collection of those which I — and other readers — seem to have enjoyed the most, starting with the astonishing confession of Soo, superstar panda of the Sooty Show, of her impending motherhood.

Some of these pieces shocked the nation — the sinister theft of Britain's garden gnomes, the dastardly plot by a bank to introduce musical cash machines, the Finns' power-crazed takeover bid for Santa Claus.

Some proved prophetic. Months after I warned that the Earth was surrounded by an orbiting ring of garbage, an expensive French satellite crashed into it and destroyed itself.

Some gave hard-headed practical advice — how to make up an excuse, how to tell gossip, how to shave, how to discover if you are fit to own a cat.

All of them were intended to give pleasure: I hope that they did.

With a few exceptions all of these pieces were published in The Mail On Sunday between 1993 and 1996. Some contain a few extra jokes. The last, called Thanks For The Memory, is much longer than the version which appeared in the newspaper. During 1996 I appeared three times on BBC Television's Mastermind. Many people asked me what it was like to walk to that black chair: that piece is my best answer.

My thanks to Jonathan Holborow, Editor of The Mail On Sunday, for his support for my column and for this collection. My thanks to all The Mail On Sunday staff who get my column oven-ready each week without losing any of the seasoning.

Richard Heller London October 1996

Contents

That's Entertainment ...

THE row over unmarried mothers took a new twist when a well-known television personality announced that she was about to become one.

Ms Soo Panda shocked the nation when she refused to name the father of the child she is expecting. Ms Panda is the long-time companion of mega-star Sooty. But she has also been seen in public on the arm of Sooty's TV rival, Sweep. Neither Ms Panda nor her agent Mr Corbett, who has handled the star throughout her career, gave any hint that either might be the father. But both confirmed that she has no plans for marriage.

Government and opposition immediately clashed over Ms Panda.

The Tory MP for Toytown, Mr Arthur Woodentop, condemned the cuddly star. He said "Thousands of teddy bears, rocking horses and even ex-service toy soldiers are living in miserable housing in over-crowded boxes, cupboards and attics. It is disgraceful that this pampered panda should jump the queue for re-housing just by getting herself pregnant."

But Labour spokeswoman, Ms Goody Twoshoes, hit back. "This is just a pretext for the government to attack the poor and the Welfare State while continuing to panda to mega-rich tax dodgers like Sonic The Hedgehog."

A fresh row broke out when an official from the much-criticised Child Support Agency revealed that both Sooty and Sweep could be made to take a DNA test. If either proved to be the father he would be made to pay "appropriate and regular maintenance". He added: "we shall look very carefully at his lifestyle. If someone is living in a luxury glovebox he can clearly afford a sizeable contribution." Other official sources added to the controversy. A Home Office statistician said that there was 'a significant link' between lone-parent pandas and crime. They were 70 per cent more likely to rob a Chinese take-away than the offspring of stable relationships like Barbie and Ken. A Scotland Yard source claimed that lone-parent pandas often played truant from playschool and were being recruited on the streets.

Immigration officials announced an inquiry into Soo's status. "She came here as a Chinese national, claiming to be joining her fiancé'. She hasn't married him and she has been working without a permit. She appears to be in breach of the controls. And unless the baby's father, or grandparents, turn out to be British he or she has no right of abode here either."

Religious leaders entered the fray when the Council of the Mammal Moral Majority demanded that Soo be sacked from her television spot, saying "This is a black and white issue. An unmarried pregnant panda sets a terrible example to impressionable children." But Archbishops Caring and Have-goodthoughts called for tolerance and compassion. "We must break down the bamboo curtain of prejudice and accept that we are a multi-species society." Former Speaker, Viscount Tonypanda, called for order, order and several MPs and peers promptly asked for a double Scotch.

In a hard-hitting speech the Prince of Wales said that far too many pandas were forced to live in high-rise mountains. Such conditions, he said, were appalling. "They open up a Panda's Box of social ills."

The pandamonium was finally brought to an end by Hello! magazine. "In her Chi-chi town house, TV's Soo shares with us the first pictures of her furry bundle of joy. 'I want to be a hands-up mother', says the overjoyed star." A nation said Aaah!

***

DANNY Baker, Bob Hoskins and the Orange Zombie have every right to protest. Their advertisements for Daz, British Telecom and Tango have been judged the most boring to appear on television. They lead a list of ten in a survey of viewers by Marketing magazine, pursued (tediously) by Persil, Guinness and Tampax. The survey is built on a fatal paradox. If an advertisement were truly boring, no viewer would remember it at all.

To meet this difficulty, the magazine could easily have used a state-of-the-art scientific method of measuring televisual boredom, developed at the Geoff Boycott Research Institute.

Viewers are placed a room which contains nothing but a television screen and a Belgian telephone directory. The survey then measures, for each programme, the average time they take to switch from the screen to the directory.

Typical survey results are: party political broadcast 15 seconds; Channel Four 'world cinema' movie 27 seconds; test card 78 seconds; nature documentary on cute meerkats 7 hours; Jeremy Beadle no reading possible (too many viewers threw directory at screen).

Even if it had found the most boring television advertisements the Marketing survey would prove little.

There is no relationship between the interest of an advertisement and the success of the product.

Anyone my age (backing towards fifty) can still remember the cigarette one was never alone with, and the guy who was never without one — a blend of Humphrey Bogart, James Dean and Marlon Brando. Millions of people wanted to be that guy (or his lover or mother): none of them bought the brand. Strand cigarettes are now one with Nineveh and Tyre.

More recently, the case of a best-selling author shows that there is no need to be afraid of boredom in advertising.

The late Marshal Kim-Il Sung of North Korea had no need of subtlety to shift his works in his own country. His campaign was monotonous but effective: Buy The Latest Kim Il-Sung Or Else...

In stark contrast were the advertisements he placed in British newspapers. They reached levels of fantasy never attempted for any other product — showing the Beloved Leader making crops grow, curing all known diseases and causing the sun to rise in the East on a daily basis.

In spite of their obvious appeal, these advertisements did little for Kim's British sales. Jeffrey Archer did not tremble.

There was even a time in American advertising when boredom was a virtue, and regarded as a sign of integrity. Products were promoted precisely for being dull and worthy.

Politicians tried to exploit the mood: one even won his party's Presidential nomination with the slogan He Dares To Be Cautious.

The test for any advertisement is not whether it is boring or fascinating but whether it tells you — quickly — something you really want to know about the product.

On that basis I nominate as the best-ever advertisement one created in a novel by Sir Kingsley Amis, although sadly no one has yet dared to use it.

It read: So-and-So's Beer MAKES YOU DRUNK!

***

I AM entirely in sympathy with the members of Equity, the actors' trade union, who have formed a pressure group called Far and Away.

Far and Away is where they would like Australian soap opera stars to be during the English pantomime season. They are sick and tired of seeing these people taking roles in our traditional Christmas theatre.

Me too. I have nothing against Australian soap stars in their place (ie Australia). I have nothing against McDonald's hamburgers in their place, but I do not expect to see them served in Simpson's-In-The-Strand in place of the roast beef of England.

If the Australian takeover is unchecked we shall surrender a priceless piece of our heritage (and put some of our best-loved actors out of work). Jack And The Beanstalk will be turned into Jason Up A Gum Tree. Mother Goose will become Mother Strewth. Dick Whittington And His Cat will be modernized into Don Bradman And His Bat.

There are some institutions which are distinctly and uniquely British. As a writer, performer and victim of pantomimes for over twenty years, I can confirm that pantomime is one of them.

It is a theatrical phenomenon which other nationalities should not attempt to gatecrash or even understand.

Take, for example, the Pantomime Dame. Must we hand all these roles over to Edna Everage? For shame. There is nothing like a (British) dame. It takes a red-blooded British male actor to put on a tutu and a bra and sing 'Nobody Loves A Fairy When She's Forty'! Could Jason Donovan do that number in a tutu? I think not.

And what of the Principal Boy? This by long tradition is played by a buxom thigh-slapping British actress. It adds a unique sexual chemistry when the Principal Boy and the Heroine sing 'If You Were The Only Boy In The World'. Can one imagine Kylie Minogue — even the new up-front-strut-your-stuff model — as Prince Charming planting a smacker on Cinderella? Madonna, just possibly, but Kylie? Do me a favour.

British pantomime demands not only a particular type of casting but a unique style of acting. Classical training and years of stagecraft, not to mention massive nerve, are needed before anybody could deliver the outrageous scripts and perform the appalling business which are the essentials of pantomime art. Could anyone but a British actor say 'winter draws on' (and would anyone but a British audience let him escape alive)?

"Hullo, Buttons, off for a swim?"

"Yes, I usually take them off for a swim".

"Well, if it isn't Dick Whittington! And if it isn't Dick Whittington I'm in the wrong theatre. I say, is that your pussy?"

Try putting them into Strine.

And in the shipboard scene, only a British sea captain would dare give out the repeated order "Avast behind!"

British pantomime has already been contaminated by television. There are far too many imported comedians who simply perform their tele-routine with no pretence of playing a pantomime character (and often with no attempt to adapt their material to a child audience). There are too many 'sports personalities', if you know what I mean, blocking traditional roles that need a traditional actor.

If the Australians take over pantomime the victory of television will be complete.

When you see the Ugly Sisters help Cinderella with the housework and start singing 'Neighbours, everybody needs good neighbours...' the final collapse of British culture cannot be far behind.

***

BRIGHTON Council is considering — seriously — a proposal that buskers should be controlled on the basis of their musical ability.

At the top end of the scale, a struggling string quartet would be allowed to charm coins from commuters with open-air Vivaldi.

But the three-chord-trick guitarist who tortures Bob Dylan would be moved smartly away or even hauled before the magistrate for a short, F-sharp shock sentence ("I would lock you up and throw away the key, if I knew which one you were playing in...")

Brighton's proposal might well require buskers to audition for the Council. Given the methods of local government, each style of music would attract its own separate sub-committee with its own specialist staff. In no time at all the Council would be advertising posts for Folk Inspectors, Reggae Co-ordinators and Easy Listening Outreach Workers. (And surely it should be promoting Brighton Rock?)

In the private sector, busker auditions would of course be conducted by one hard-bitten agent in a raincoat. He or she would give each performer a maximum of fifteen seconds, before saying "Leave your name — but not with me."

Brighton Council could knock out many buskers with some simple rules. Strictly no harmonicas. Strictly no bongos. No sound systems (a busker should have the confidence and talent to hack it as a live musician). No Elvis impersonators — unless they can *prove* that they are the real Elvis.

Many people assume that the word 'busker' is modern and has something to do with 'bus queue'. It is in fact Victorian, from an era when street musicians had a strong sense of craft and calling.

They dealt fiercely with poor performers and reserved the most lucrative sites for good musicians. One specially-favoured passage leading out of Waterloo Station was occupied by the same fiddler for his entire career — truly a case of putting all your busks in one exit.

This traditional system has broken down. Now *anyone* can try to be a busker, with no need for ability or apprenticeship. The absolute worst, the pits of the orchestra, are the ones who go *inside* moving public transport.

These wretches, who prey on the captive passengers of a bus or a train, usually proceed in pairs — one to strum and warble, his mate to say "good afternoon, sir" (or 'Missus') in a leering, suggestive manner. The mate will often offer "alternative comedy" — an expression which would be more accurate with the extra word 'to' inside it.

This kind of performance is not busking. It is aural assault and extortion, and counter-measures are clearly required. Buses and trains should be equipped with an extra emergency anti-busking button, whose touch would fill the air with 'My Way' at full karaoke volume. Passengers might also care to purchase a new special spray — Buskrot — guaranteed to shrivel guitar strings at a range of ten metres.

Buskers apprehended in buses and trains should be give deterrent sentences — transportation might be appropriate.

However, in all fairness, the law should crack down equally fiercely on *everybody* who forces people to listen to unwanted tunes in a public place.

Live or recorded — what's the difference? Piped music should be made an arrestable offence.

***

ONE of the world's greatest plays was recently re-written for an English local council.

Anton Chekhov created for 'The Cherry Orchard' a minor character called Yasha, a manservant with pretentious tastes.

He smokes an obnoxious cigar on stage, to which other characters react.

However, the cigar has now been banned by the licensing authority of Stratford district council. In the recent Royal Shakespeare Company production, Mark Lockyer, the actor playing Yasha, was obliged to mime the cigar while the other characters complained about his non-existent smoke.

In nearly a hundred years, no known production of 'The Cherry Orchard' has caused a theatre fire, and the RSC's Swan Theatre had taken every possible precaution against Yasha's dangerous embers. The ban can hardly be justified on safety grounds, and one can only assume that it is politically motivated.

If so, it is surprising that the council stopped at Yasha's cigar. There are so many other 'incorrect' things in 'The Cherry Orchard' which should have been blue-pencilled.

The character of the successful peasant-entrepreneur, Lopakhin, drinks a lot of kvass (fermented rye beer) — a clear incitement to alcoholism. The council should insist on a new line for Lopakhin: "this no-alcohol kvass tastes great, and leaves me a clear head for property deals with feckless aristocrats."

Another character is a senile manservant called Firs, babbling of the past — a cruel portrait of Alzheimer's disease. This character must either be transformed into a sharp-witted, wise-cracking George Burns figure or written out of the play.

Above all, the council will have to fix the terrible ending of 'The Cherry Orchard' — beautiful, historic trees being chopped down by a developer. Oh no! In a new dénouement, the trees could be saved by a heroic commune of New Age protesters.

Mind you, I do not know how Stratford council has lived with a chauvinist reactionary like Shakespeare for so many years. I am amazed that it has not insisted on a new low-fat Falstaff, or inserted the number of the local Samaritans into Hamlet's famous soliloquy.

It should long ago have re-written The Taming Of The Shrew as The Taming Of The Slob. In this version, Petruchio could become a house-husband while a still-assertive Katherina fulfils herself in the media and becomes editor of the Padua Sunday Exsuccess.

Such an overhaul of Shakespeare has its precedents. In the early nineteenth century Professor Bowdler entered the English language by producing a sanitized version of the plays with none of their unnecessary indecencies. Before him, Nahum Tate re-wrote King Lear with a happy ending.

In their time, these versions were regarded as definitive. They are now regarded as asinine, examples of the folly of imposing the standards of a different age on a genius.

Stratford council joins Tate and Bowdler at its peril. To return to Chekhov: one of his greatest strengths, like Dickens, was to bring minor characters to life with tiny details. If he wanted a cigar-smoking manservant he knew what he was doing.

So light up, Yasha, and lighten up, Stratford!

***

HATS off to Barbara and Ken Follett! The Labour party's principal stylist and her author husband have found a solution to Britain's unemployment problem.

They maintain a 'Follett Office' to propel them through their busy lives. Their stationery identifies them (coyly, by first name only) as Terri, Executive Secretary, Pam, Press and Diary, Victor, Information Technology and Ann, Follett Trust.

This 'Fab Four' is only a beginning. In a few month's time, Parkinson's Law will see them multiply into a beehive.

No one can be styled an 'Executive Secretary' without the accompaniment of at least a 'Deputy Secretary'. Terri will be soon be joined by June, and since neither could be expected to make beverages or answer the telephone, April and May cannot be far behind. Pam's job must in the course of nature split like an amoeba into its constituent parts, and Victor alone cannot conceivably keep pace with the rapidly changing world of information technology. More help wanted...

Since Barbie and Ken are two people, with widely varied

needs and demands, all of these assistants can eventually expect to be doubled and re-organized into a B division and a K division. Each of these will require a divisional manager, and probably a deputy (with support staff), and they in turn will require co-ordination by a group manager with a seat on the board.

I have especially high hopes for that 'Follett Trust'. No self-respecting trust can work without grants officers, outreach teams, evaluation officers, and of course fund-raisers: Ann shall have Brenda and Camilla and Diana ... and Xanthe and Yolande and Zoe.

A workforce of this size will of course require the services of personnel managers, payroll officers, caterers, health and safety supervisors, equal opportunities observers and European Union compliance officers. At any given time, many of them will be on leave for maternity, paternity, study, sport or sheer joie de vivre, and will require the services of a substitute.

As caring socialists, pardon me, stakeholders, Barbie and Ken will wish to provide their staff with personal trainers, stress counsellors and of course, a works council.

This new army of employees, each with a statutory entitlement to minimum personal space, will stretch the accommodation resources of Follett Towers and the consequent move to new premises will engender fresh employment for real estateniks, removers, installers — and still more stress counsellors.

Although I cannot hope to match the Folletts, their efforts have inspired me to create a few extra jobs of my own.

I now employ a Stationery Buyer. I actually buy no stationery whatever, but having somebody else to answer the endless, importunate telephone calls of Stationery Salespeople will generate immense savings of time, energy and peace of mind.

To save wear on my heartstrings, I am employing a Charity Officer (Mr E Scrooge) to refuse all begging letters. Letters from creditors are now answered by two highly-qualified staff, Mr Harold Skimpole and Mr Wilkins Micawber.

Preparation of this column is now assisted by several specialists. Puns are now supplied by Mr Luke Upward (try that name again, slowly), who was sadly made redundant in the recent slump in the Christmas cracker industry. Irony is handled by our Mr Swift and in the Metaphor Division I expect great things from our Youth Trainee, Mr Amis. A former French polisher, M Flaubert, gives a sheen to my sentences.

However, for really demanding literary tasks I employ only the best. I am therefore delighted to announce the recruitment of Miss Joan Collins.

***

CIVIL liberties took a giant leap forward with the recent decision that a man may not be sacked for wearing black suede cowboy boots with evening dress.

A trombonist, Mr Kenneth Shifrin, won £10,000 compensation from the City of Birmingham Symphony Orchestra, which dismissed him after detecting the offending pair during a performance in Poland.

The historic 'trombone case' almost certainly turned on Mr Shifrin's claim that the orchestra's conductor, Sir Simon Rattle, was himself a habitual wearer of black suede shoes in performance.

Conductors, who work standing up, may well feel that they deserve more liberty in this department than their seated subordinates. On health grounds, many would be well advised to perform in suitable training shoes. The late Leonard Bernstein, famous for his leaps at the podium, could have signed a lucrative contract with Nike.

However, if a Polish audience could stand without swooning or rioting the sight of a British conductor in black suede shoes it was unreasonable for the orchestra to object to the virtually invisible footwear of its trombonist.

More disturbingly, Mr Shifrin won a further victory in a dispute over his trousers. They had zips on the pockets. Here the orchestra had a point. Cowboy boots may be condoned, but zippered pockets are beyond the pale after sunset. If only Mr Shifrin had employed a gentleman's personal gentleman:

Jeeves would have left a hot iron on the offending garments rather than let them be worn in public.

It would be tragic if the case let musicians wear anything they like. Nigel Kennedy has already done enough to earn incarceration in a maximum sartorial prison.

Years ago the comedian Robin Williams created an imaginary squad of Taste Police, with powers of immediate arrest for people wearing polyester. Such a force may be needed to cope with a complete breakdown in law and wardrobe. If a trombonist gets away with black suede, how soon will we see triangle players in florescent socks?

However, it would be more in keeping with British traditions if the Royal Family resumed its role as arbiters of style. Edward VII was famous for his landmark judgments, as when he upbraided the Earl of Malmesbury for wearing tweeds at a race meeting: "Going ratting, Harris?"

Apart from his taste in clothes, Mr Shifrin was alleged to have irritated a French horn player by moving his music stand. Happily, this allegation was unproven. French horn players are notoriously nervous nellies, who deserve a helping hand. No one would wish them tormented by brass bullies in their section.

Not just musicians, but all employees are entitled to protection at work against deliberate or reckless disturbance from nearby objects. In an open-plan office, someone who incessantly moves a chair, or rattles a teacup and saucer, or even rustles papers, can make it impossible for a colleague to concentrate or take a nap.

Worse still are the compulsive window-opener (who invariably attracts the compulsive window-shutter), the drummer on the desk (whether he uses a ruler or just bare fingers), the amateur cricketer (who perpetually throws and misses at the wastepaper basket) and the person who changes other peoples' calendars.

While wishing Mr Shifrin well in his future career, I hope that none of these people will take encouragement from his victory. Trombonists in cowboy boots are all very well — but no one could endure a nation of fiddlers.

***

AFTER bending a million spoons, paranormalist Uri Geller, like Alexander of old, has sought fresh worlds to conquer.

He now claims to be able to project thought-waves into theatre critics. Unknown to them, he was in the first-night audience of Martin Sherman's play 'Some Sunny Day', sending out positive vibrations.

Although the critics generally agreed that the play was incomprehensible, most of them gave it excellent reviews.

One admirer, Charles Spencer of The Daily Telegraph, referred to the inexplicably good frame of mind in which he wrote his first-night notice — relaxed and calm instead of his usual panic. Although he found it 'preposterous' he called Some Sunny Day "one of the most entertaining and unexpected plays of the year."

Needless to say, The Mail On Sunday's David Hughes was able to keep his head when others were losing theirs. He praised the superb actors, including Corin Redgrave, Cheryl Campbell and Rupert Everett, while recording firmly 'Collapse of play'.

But even he used a phrase which suggested the invisible influence of Mr Geller: "you can scarcely keep your mind on the message."

In the good old days, theatre and concert managers had a much simpler method of inducing calm and relaxation. They plied reviewers with drink.

This offered reliable guidance to the general public. The quality of a review could be related, quite simply, to the time that it was composed. A glowing review meant a glowing critic — after three drinks in the first interval. A stinking review meant that the critic had seen the whole play and consequently acquired a hangover.

An ecstatic review implied a critic too fuddled to do more than dictate a hand-out from the management.

One such hack produced a legendary notice in 'The Irish Times' of a recital by the great Polish pianist Paderewski. After reading over his hand-out, he revived sufficiently to add an insight of his own: "Mr Paderewski gave a most musicianly rendition of the above items, and was observed to play with equal facility on the black notes as on the white."

It would be no surprise to hear that Uri Geller has been at work on the world's art critics. That would explain why so many of them demand admiration for displays of dead animals, or artists' bodily wastes, or (quite literally) piles of rubbish, and why their language is so often 'paranormally' pretentious and obscure. But it is shocking to think that he could 'bend' such a clear-minded, no-nonsense bunch as our drama critics.

A night out at the theatre is an expensive business. Play-goers are entitled to dependable reviews. If something is described as 'a magical evening' the magic should come from the play and the actors, not a paranormal persuader secreted in the audience.

Our theatre critics should not be allowed to attend a first night without a spoon in their pockets. If it starts bending, they should walk out at once and insist on strong drink from the management.

Whatever he does to critics, it is heartening to discover that Mr Geller has no influence on the general public.

In spite of his good vibrations, Some Sunny Day closed after two months.

***

POLAND is the nation of Chopin. It was once ruled by a concert pianist, Paderewski. Its cultural destiny is now in the hands of Mr Malcolm McLaren, best known in musical history as manager of the Sex Pistols, featuring Johnny Rotten and the late Sid Vicious.

He has been recruited by Poland's new President, Mr Kwasniewski, to help give the country a new and sophisticated image — Polish with polish.

To be fair, Mr McLaren has for some years been trying to live down his past life as the Prince of Punk and the Apostle of Anti-Fashion. He even claims to have written "a cowboy musical about Oscar Wilde" (did it feature a country-and-western Ballad of Reading Gaol?)

He began his assignment foolishly with an assault on Polish cuisine. He asked Poles to give up dumplings, pig's trotters and grey meat floating in borsch and switch to noodles.

This is a silly and unnatural idea. The Poles invented these hearty dishes to cater for the rigours of their climate. If Mr McLaren really wants them to eat wisps of pasta instead, he should move the whole country south, stopping only at the Mediterranean or the Black Sea.

Worse still, he apparently sees the noodle as the first step towards converting the Poles to Japanese food.

No country deserves such a terrible conquest. Japanese food is simply an exquisitely beautiful excuse to serve a very small helping. As for sushi ... it has everything you hate seeing when you go out snorkelling assembled for you on a plate. After one month of Nipponese nibbles the Poles will be whimpering for pig's trotters.

Mr McLaren also has designs on Poland's furniture. He claims that the Poles favour fake leather armchairs and objects made from crushed Coca-Cola cans. Well, why not? That is a fine blend of comfort, ecology and pop iconography. With his Japanese proclivities, Mr McLaren will no doubt try to force them to adopt the futon — the sofa-bed specially designed to prevent people from either sitting down or falling asleep.

He would do better to target Poland's currency: the zloty. It is depressing for any country to use money which rhymes with grotty or snotty. He should rename it the Happy, divided into 100 Yummies: money which creates a Feel-Good Factor.

Another problem for Poland's image is its alphabet. Its letters are full of strange squiggles (the technical term is diacritical marks.) These are very unpopular with printers and make Polish names a trap to the consonantally-challenged (it took us fifteen years to get Walesa right and now the Poles have thrown him out). Mr McLaren should declare Death to Dire Criticals and give the Poles exciting new Western spellings like Kwik, or Eezi, or Overnite.

Whatever Mr McLaren achieves in Poland, it would be depressing and sinister if his function were duplicated in Britain.

The last thing we need from any government is a Secretary of State for Style, with a supporting cast of junior ministers, officials and inspectors. Before long these people would demand enforcement powers. "Police in Scunthorpe today arrested five people on suspicion of wearing flares. Meanwhile Customs officers at Dover seized a lorry-load of pictures of kittens, described by a spokesman as hardcore cute."

A Ministry of Style would be a threat to democracy as well as civil liberty. How many people could afford to change their government if they then had to change all their furniture?

***

IN A humane and artistic gesture the BBC National Orchestra of Wales is to give away boiled sweets to its audiences. It hopes to stop them coughing during performances.

The orchestra may remember the infamous first night of 'Carmen' which was wrecked when the audience strummed their catarrhs. But its bid to put harmony in place of cacoughony could easily misfire.

The continuous unwrapping of the sweets will be almost as irritating as the noise it seeks to prevent. Still more annoying will be the whispered bids of spectators to swap flavours.

Sweet addicts could even hold the orchestra to ransom and secure an extra issue by threatening to hack during an adagio. And why stop at sweets? By adding sneezes and nose-blowing to their repertoire, unscrupulous patrons could try to extort a free hot-whisky-and-lemon at the first interval.

The orchestra should recognize that some works are actually improved by coughing. The average cougher has a range of two octaves and a trained soprano or baritone can easily extend this beyond three. If added to the pertussin section of the orchestra, professional coughers could provide extra rhythm and brio to say, Tchaikovsky's 1812 Overture or Verdi's Grand March from Aïda.

Musicians are not the only people who should stop audience noise. Cinema proprietors should provide all-day gobstoppers to inhibit talking during film performances.

No film ever made — not even 'Escape Of The Killer Tomatoes' — has been improved by dialogue from the audience, such as "I've been there" or "I've seen him, he used to be in Crossroads."

The biggest gobstoppers of all should be given to graduates of film schools.

These people cannot go to a film (they will always pretentiously call it a 'movie' whether or not they are American) without explaining it shot by shot, just loud enough to compete with the actors. They constantly compare the film on the screen (which you have paid to watch) with a completely different one which you have not chosen to watch. They can find a quotation from Ingemar Bergman in the middle of 'Toy Story'.

Apart from silencing talkers, gobstoppers could also suppress noisy kissers in the back rows. To be fair, these performers are often more convincing than those in the film, but it is literally a pain in the neck to turn round and watch them instead.

Best of all, gobstoppers could replace all the other loud food and drink in cinemas — things which are perversely designed to crunch, slurp, rustle or rattle when consumed.

It is ironic that cinemas which crack down so fiercely on passive smoking should have invented the curse of passive eating. If dropped from the air on an enemy population the odour of cinema popcorn would be outlawed under the Geneva Convention.

Talkers and eaters in an audience may be incorrigible, but coughers and sneezers might think of their own self-interest.

They should not waste such wonderful symptoms in a concert or theatre or cinema. They should use them only in their place of work, loudly and often until somebody says "You sound terrible. You should go home right away."

Love And Marriage

NOW will you please raise your screens to Dawn and Dragan, the first couple to be married on the Internet?

Art student Dawn Raid (clearly a keen follower of newspaper headlines) exchanged vows with graphic artist Dragan Radosavlevich in a 'cybercafe' in central London. They were connected by screen to their minister, Rev Jonathan Blake — who had never met them — officiating from a similar establishment several miles away.

Internet weddings are an excellent idea. Churches have been "service — providers" for centuries, and it is a logical next step to turn themselves into Wedsites. The Church of England could easily amend some of its traditional Frequently Asked Questions. "Wilt thou surf with no other? Wilt thou now download this thy partner, in real time, as long as ye both shall browse?"

On-line marriage would also be an immense convenience to guests, freeing them from all the ordeals of a traditional wedding.

For starters, no more expeditions to the Polar regions of department stores to consult the 'bride's book'. No more horrifying revelations of the couple's taste in china, glassware and duvet covers. Above all, no depressing discovery that all the cheapest items have already been ordered by other people.

Internet wedding lists will of course be accessible on-line. Guests will dial up the couple's page, say http://wedmary.john/lootlist and can send something without even having to look at it. Reluctant guests could add the instruction //tightwad, and the computer would confine its search to bargain-basement tea towels or oil-and-vinegar cruets.

On-line wedding guests would not have to buy frocks and

hats. They would not have to watch their partners buying frocks and hats (nor say the fatal words "I liked you best in the first one"). Having finally bought a frock and hat, the wearer would not discover their doubles on the guest she cannot stand.

Nor would on-screen wedding guests have to hire morning dress. They would not have to hear their waist measurements shouted in front of their horrified partners. They would not be mistaken for catering staff at the wedding reception.

An on-line wedding reception has no warm champagne or chilled sandwiches, no melting canapés or concrete cake. Guests are not obliged to listen to speeches — by a silly-ass Hugh Grant best man, or even worse, by the interminable friend of the bride's family. They could read these things on screen if they choose, but if they see the opening line "Ladies and gentlemen, it gives me great pleasure and it has done for many years…" they can wipe out the next awful half-hour.

On-line wedding guests would also be spared the familiar nightmare of meeting somebody they know they know but have forgotten.

They would not have to make desperate conversation in a search for clues to the identity of the other party, "How are your parents these days? Still doing the same thing?" "Yes, still Queen and Duke of Edinburgh."

Convenient as they are, on-line weddings do carry certain risks. Internet users frequently employ multiple fantasy personalities, and this opens ominous scope for cybigamy. The on-line minister should forestall this by asking: "if any user knows any just cause why these two persons should not be joined, let him or her e-mail now or forever disconnect…"

A couple who marry on-line might enjoy a virtual-reality honeymoon. If he preferred Venice, and she wanted the Seychelles, they could both get their wish and neither would meet a mosquito. They might thereafter prefer a 'virtual marriage', sharing a site but not a sitting-room.

But the information revolution cannot provide a substitute for one marital activity. Although cyberweddings may become fashionable, there will be no demand for cyberchristenings.

***

EXPERTS were (you guessed it) 'baffled' by the Barclays computer which handles mortgage and loans to the bank's staff. Suddenly it stopped making payments to all employees named Fiona.

The fault was quickly contained and corrected and the stricken Fionas are sleeping safely again under their indebted roofs. But the bank cannot explain the outbreak of Fiphobia.

The obvious suspect is a computer-programmer who has been jilted by one of the bank's Fionas. But the bank claims that no one like that could access its system, and why would the rejected Romeo take such a limited revenge? Having hacked that far, he could surely have fired all the Fionas, or transferred them all to Barclays in Stornaway? And why stick to Fiona? Even a dimwit would have included all the bank's Sharons and Traceys to lay false trails for the investigators.

Barclays has preferred to blame its computer, and well it might. Clearing bank computers make mistakes all the time. The one I deal with tells me regularly that I have no money at all — a mirror-image of the error made by the Inland Revenue's, which believes that I have lashings of it.

If Chancellor Kenneth Clarke really wants to bring the 'feel-good' factor back to the British economy, he should simply order the banks and the Inland Revenue to swap computers.

Amazingly enough, both explanations for the attack on Fiona are true. It was the work of a lovesick computer — possessed by a doomed passion for a distant acronym.

Ever since HAL went haywire in '2001' we have known that computers can suffer from emotional overload. The latest victim was a humble computer named ELMER, Barclays' Employee Loans and Mortgages EncodeR.

Day after day he fantasized about his distant goddess, the bank's central, state-of-the-art, FInancial ON-line Algorithmic computer: FIONA. He invited her out on computer dates. She turned them all down. She would not even join him for a quick byte in the electronic canteen. He sent her bigger and bigger parcels of data. She did not even acknowledge.

Finally he tried a desperate interface. "I'm not even a peripheral to you! You haven't got the tiniest memory of me!" At last FIONA noticed him. Her enraged circuits blazed out the terrible command: "De-access!"

Spurned and humiliated, ELMER had but one thought — to punish every Fiona within his power...

Such electronic melodramas are likely to become more common with the new generation of 'neural' computers, whose systems simulate a biological brain. They have something close to imagination: they can cope with unexpected information and can 'learn' to adapt and even create their own programmes.

One of these new systems is even thought capable of writing scripts or books. An early experiment in this field is most promising. Given only a data bank of metaphors to work from, without the benefit of character, dialogue or plot, the computer wrote a Martin Amis novel in thirty seconds without even asking for an advance.

But if computers are treated like artists they will soon award themselves the right to display artistic temperament. When that happens, I am putting my money into the first bank to bring back the abacus.

***

NO sex scandal has reached lower depths than the story of the two octopuses who were found by an American marine scientist making love to each other on the seabed 8000 feet below the surface of the Pacific Ocean.

The scientist, Dr Richard Lutz, was amazed to discover that both were male.

His colleague, Dr Janet Voight, has suggested that they were sex-starved and unable to find a female.

But her theory has drawn a bitter protest from one of the octopuses.

"It's nothing to do with a shortage of females," he told me. "The fact is I'm gay and proud of it! Dr Voight is just showing off her speciesism and phobic prejudices. Does she think that only a homo sapiens can be a homosexual?"

Identifying himself only as Orlando, he inked in for me the moving details of the life that has turned him and his lover, Oscar, into the outcasts of the ocean.

There is nothing to mark Orlando as different from any other octopus. He is straight-acting and a star forward in underwater hockey, who could have turned professional. Instead he became the idol of his weekend team. Other octopuses would compete for the privilege of buying him a pint of plankton after matches.

But then they found out about Oscar. His team shunned him. "They were afraid to get in the shower with me. It's crazy! I've never had tentacles for anyone but Oscar.

"I think I knew I was gay when I was only a little mollusc. But I always thought I'd grow out of it. But then I saw Oscar. He was playing a string quartet — all by himself. I knew then that I would never love another octopus."

The two lovers live in a poky flat in a low-rise tower block at the bottom of a trench. Oscar supports them both from his earnings as a musician: Orlando lost his job as a traffic policeman. "We don't go out much. Most evenings we watch David Attenborough videos. If we have time we hug each other — just you try finding places for sixteen arms.

"When that scientist caught us it was the first time we had been out for weeks.

"Why couldn't he leave us alone? We're both adults, we're both consenting and you'd think eight thousand feet under is private enough!"

Orlando told me that many other marine creatures are gay or bisexual, and surprised me by naming several celebrities. "Flipper the dolphin? When did you see him with a girl friend? And as for Jaws... Off the movie set that one's a different kettle of fish or should I say, a different fettle of kitsch? Killer shark? Forget it. Camp as a Bedouin hotel convention. Turns into the Drag Queen Of The Depths, more fruit than Carmen Miranda..."

Suddenly Orlando seized my hands in his tentacles. I felt distinctly outnumbered. "Don't worry," he squirted. "I just hope you understand now. That's all we want, us octogays. Understanding, not favours or special treatment. Some day I hope we will be able to come out of the water closet."

I asked him if he had any regrets about choosing Oscar. "Non! Rien de rien!" came the instant reply. "I know I could have had an easier life by pretending to be straight. But I guess I'm just a sucker for love!"

(published for the first time)

***

TAKE with the largest pinch of salt you can find the 'discovery' by the latest British sex survey that men are far more likely to be adulterers than women.

After questioning 19,000 men and women about their sexual record over five years, the Wellcome Trust found that one in twenty wives admitted to adultery. The rate for husbands was higher — rising to one in ten among the professional classes.

This simply reflects the fact that men are far more boastful than women. Jack The Lad is an archetype: Jill The Lass is a rarity.

At the same time, men are far more insecure about their waning sexual attractions and powers. The older they get, the more they need to prop up their self-image as objects of desire.

Put these two ingredients together, and one can see why older husbands would tell a sympathetic investigator that they are adulterers. It offers the same relief as a telephone sex-line, and it is free. It is an absolute certainty that many husbands' 'confessions' are unfulfilled fantasies, and I would suggest that the survey studies the statistical relationship between the number of such confessions and the size of the husband's paunch, the recession of his hairline and the number of his teeth.

However, the survey did produce a genuine surprise. It

found that high-earning professional husbands were five times readier to admit to (or brag about) adultery than married male manual workers. Truly, A Tale Of Two Suits: double-breasted means double-dealer, but a boiler-suit hides a faithful heart.

The survey offered no explanation for this divergence. I suspect that it is simple: successful professional husbands are trying to emulate the traditional behaviour of the English aristocracy, for whom adultery was as natural a pursuit as fox-hunting. Witness all those part-time husbands and full-time cads latterly televised in Edith Wharton's The Buccaneers.

Whatever its explanation the arrival of professional adultery is a deeply serious development. The professional classes are the drivers and determinants of social behaviour and public morals. They have the power to make clothes, foods, holidays, film directors and politicians fashionable: they can do the same for sin.

If left unchecked and unrepentant, professional men will turn adultery into *aspirational behaviour*, something done for status rather than passion. Filing clerks will check floozies into hotels in the hope of being taken for libel lawyers or derivatives dealers.

Professional attitudes have already overturned the traditional concept of the Seven Deadly Sins. These are now rigidly demarcated: some sins are for high-flyers, others for under-achievers.

The In-Sins are Lust, Pride and Envy. They combine a healthy respect for one's own attractions and possessions with a wholly desirable wish to exceed those of others. The Out-Sins are Gluttony and Sloth (which should be purged at the gym, society's new secular temple) and Anger (a seriously unfashionable sin, especially if performed solo on public transport). Definitely on the way down since the Eighties is Avarice, now acceptable only in the form of Tax Avoidance.

The Wellcome Trust investigators did confirm the strength of one traditional pattern of behaviour among all classes, including the professionals. About 80 per cent of those surveyed claimed to believe that sex outside marriage was wrong.

Sins may wax and wane, but hypocrisy endures for ever.

***

WE all know the Wedding March, but a Gloucester couple took it several steps further by inventing the Wedding Trot.

They celebrated their recent marriage by leading over a hundred guests in a 40-minute jog around the city.

I hope that they put a warning on their wedding invitation for people to turn up with some suitable clothes. If they asked their male guests to jog through the streets of Gloucester in hired morning coats and striped trousers, and their female ones to do the same in posh frocks and high heels, they could easily have provoked mutiny and demands for return of the wedding presents.

I wonder also if the couple employed ushers along their chosen route, to count the guests in and to prevent reluctant joggers from slipping away into a pub. Slow coaches could have been hurried up by the terrible warning: "Last one home has to make a speech at the reception! Next to last has to listen to it!"

The wedding jog must have posed a challenge to the guests who wanted to play the traditional practical jokes on the happy pair.

They might have been able to slip a Just Married sign onto the back of the newlyweds' T-shirts. But even the dreamiest couple might have noticed a string of tin cans attached to their running shoes.

I feel sorry for the wedding photographer. Accustomed to lining up wedding groups in the conventional static poses, he must have found it a shock to pursue the Gloucester couple and their guests like a paparazzo snatching at Royalty. The wedding jog would also have created unusual demands for the caterers at the reception. Rarely, if ever, would they have been asked to throw water over super-heated guests (conventional weddings might benefit from this innovation in high summer).

The couple no doubt asked for a no-fat high-carbohydrate wedding cake. And in place of champagne, were they toasted in lightly-chilled Lucozade?

They were also, in all probability, the first to have their wedding gift list at a sports shop. As with all such lists, they would quickly have discovered their true friends — the ones who sent them the matching state-of-the-art his-and-hers multi-fitness machines. Cheapskates would have opted for the matching three-packs of white cotton socks.

The Gloucester wedding jog is certain to be imitated. Before long, some other couple will try to go one better and have their entire ceremony performed on the run, accompanied by a panting vicar, best man, bridesmaids, pages and guests.

Such a wedding might require a few changes in the established requests and responses. "Wilt thou take this woman, to have and to hold?"

"I will if I ever catch up with her."

A couple can jog at their wedding if they insist, but they should be forbidden to do it on their honeymoon.

Jogging is a solitary activity. Joggers rarely talk to each other. Many do not even try; instead they seal themselves away behind a personal stereo.

Honeymoons are for walking, not Walkmans, for talking rather than gasping, and for contact, not conditioning.

Honeymooners should not need to run to make their hearts beat faster.

Body And Soul

THERE has been a new flare-up in the long-running civil war between Britain's restaurants and their customers.

Sir Terence Conran, proprietor of London's elite eatery, Quaglino's, wrote a letter to a luncher complaining about his 'derisory and insulting' tip on a bill of £1800.

For many years, the civil war has been shifting in favour of restaurant-owners, through their use of surprise weapons, such as balsamic vinegar and long-range rocket salads, and shock tactics. Smoking customers have been cut off and isolated, deprived of supporting fire, and driven out of many parts of the battlefield.

Restaurant-owners were quick to see the role of communications and propaganda. Customers were confused, and their morale undermined, by menus and wine lists the length of War And Peace, which caused many to surrender unresisting to the suggestions of the waiter. Equally successful variations on this strategy were the menu illegibly chalked on a blackboard unviewable without the services of an osteopath, or the menu gabbled by a monotone maître dee at the speed of a Kentucky tobacco auction.

Most cruel of all, restaurants invented nouvelle cuisine. Besides providing the perfect excuse for serving a very small helping, it left many customers too weakened by hunger to query their bills.

Even against this background, the despatch of a letter to an unsatisfactory tipper is a serious escalation of the conflict. On a bill for £1800 it represents a demand for unconditional surrender.

Under the normal rules of engagement, the restaurant would simply have prepared for the bad tipper to return with important guests. It would then make a point of forgetting his name and have trouble tracing his booking, before placing him and the guests at the Table From Hell, the one in the flight path of the kitchen door or the lavatory. Really bad tippers would be assigned a table next to Michael Winner.

Tipping was already a minefield, but restaurants have added to its peril with the 'optional service charge'.

A friend of mine has led a fearless counter-attack against this sinister new weapon. When appropriate, he writes on the bill: "I agree. The service in this restaurant is indeed optional." (He once sent a tardy waiter a note asking if he had any plans for dinner.)

Instead of sending hostile letters to bad tippers, restaurants should look for added incentives to good ones.

They could be given extra issues of after dinner mints and/or hot towels, and a guard of honour as they leave. Scout patrols would be sent out to protect their cars from traffic wardens.

Restaurants might also invite their best tippers to submit celebrity photographs of themselves to hang on the wall, alongside all those actors and actresses who can never be identified but are vaguely remembered from appearances in British films. Superlative tippers could be allowed to scrawl a cheesy message suggesting bosom friendship with the restaurant owner. For Quaglino's this might read "To Terry-Baby, I Can't Resist That Black Forest Gateau."

Or perhaps someone could invent for restaurants the equivalent of a fairground Try-Your-Strength machine. A 'derisory and insulting' tip would send the needle only as far as 'Mr Stingy', a better one would push it up to 'Come Again' and a great one would ring bells and flash lights as 'Tip Top Tarzan'.

Should these expedients fail, restaurants could always fall back on the traditional but proven methods of good food, good helpings, good service and good manners.

**

HISTORY is bunk, said Henry Ford. Maybe so, but an Austrian court has just decided that history is copyright and that future generations can be forced to pay for it.

This startling principle underpins the judgement in favour of an American psychic, Miss Judy Knight, who uses the technique of 'channelling' to receive messages from Ramtha, an Egyptian warrior from the year 35,000 BC.

Judge Friedinger awarded her custody of Ramtha against a rival channeller, Frau Ravel, who was made to pay her £600 for spiritual piracy. The judge accepted Miss Knight's claim to have established para-psychological contact with Ramtha, which she has turned into a lucrative business at her home in Washington state.

Thousands flock there to see her sink into a deep trance and dispense ancient Egyptian wisdom in a gruff man's voice. In spite of his great age Ramtha regularly gives up-to-the-minute stock market advice. Did his customers include that Mr Leeson from Barings Bank? I think we should be told.

Without the benefit of legal training, you and I might think that 'channelling' is phoney pseudo-psycho drivel invented by people with a deep spiritual interest in other people's money.

Channellers typically claim contact with someone like Ramtha, from a totally lost civilization. That way they can never be faulted on details. Just for the record, Ramtha's alleged life in 35,000 BC would make him a contemporary of Neanderthals. It puts him some 25,000 years before the development of agriculture and over 30,000 years before the first known writing.)

But none of these arguments influenced Judge Friedinger. She pronounced Ramtha 'a spiritual entity', of whom Miss Knight could claim unique knowledge.

In the light of her ruling, I can reveal that I am the sole channel for Napoleon.

In layman's terms, I am Napoleon. He and I are like that. We talk every day. Listen, I'll tell you what went wrong at Waterloo. It was the mud. I could not get the artillery deployed until the ground dried at 9.30 am. (Next week: why I really split with Josephine.)

Napoleon is mine, I tell you, mine. Anyone who depicts him or refers to him without my permission will be hearing from my lawyers. This includes references to Napoleon brandy, the Napoleonic wars or the Napoleonic code or the bad pig in

Orwell's Animal Farm, and the use of Napoleon in any simile or metaphor whatsoever. You have been warned.

While I am at it, I think I will also channel into Beethoven. If I can bring Beethoven back to life it means that all his music goes back into copyright. I would collect 168 years of accumulated royalties. And to think that before channelling I could not even play a note.

Although Napoleon and Beethoven are taken there are still plenty of historic figures available: Alexander, Shakespeare, Michaelangelo, Felix The Cat... Would it not be wonderful to offer these and other alternative lives as special 'channelling prizes' on the National Lottery? I can see the poster now: a series of legendary faces over the slogan They Could Happen To You.

***

A REPORT, pardon me, a *shock* report, on BBC Newsnight claimed that Britain is suffering from 'an epidemic of obesity', costing the National Health Service £2 billion a year.

This figure should be taken with a pinch of salt — on top of a double portion of chips.

Ponder, please, that heavy word 'epidemic', implying that obesity is a disease. It is not, nor is it spread, like epidemics, by contact with a sufferer. It is quite safe to shake hands with a fat person or even make love to one.

Obesity is simply a label attached to certain groups of people, judged by constantly changing ideals of beauty and athleticism. (Canova's voluptuous Three Graces would now be renamed the Three Grosses and frog-marched to aerobics classes). Obesity is in the eye of the beholder (usually what the beholder sees last thing at night in the mirror, breathing in).

Attempts to measure it more scientifically are doomed to failure and cheating. I have a table of 'desirable weights' for men of my height (desirable to whom? Michelle Pfeiffer, I hope). It tells me that with a small frame I am a slob but if I have a large frame I am a Schwarzenegger. Guess which frame I award myself. And don't give me that one about pinching an inch of flesh below the fifth rib.

If you cannot *find* the fifth rib, how do you know where to pinch?

A more reliable test is that of ordering clothes in a department store. If the assistant directs you to wallpapers you may well be obese.

Statisticians are entitled to invent definitions of obesity, but they have no right to put a cost on it.

To repeat: obesity is not a disease. Many obese people are healthy and long-lived. One memorably obese Englishman made it past ninety in spite of heavy indulgence in alcohol and nicotine, and an intensely stressful occupation (war leader).

Obesity is at worst a potential contributor to disease, dis-function or premature death. For that reason a partially obese society might well be more expensive to its health services than a totally fit one.

But such a comparison is — in a word — fatuous. A totally fit society is unimaginable except in an Orwellian tyranny. Where would you rather live: a country where you have to perform physical jerks or a country where you are allowed to become one?

Obese people are not a *cost* to the nation. They are *part* of the nation and are entitled to the care of the nation's health service — as are drinkers and smokers and roller-bladers, and many other people whose lifestyle or chosen activities carry extra risks of illness or injury.

Our bodies are simply a car that we drive. Some of us drive a sleek sports car, others a sloppy saloon. The sports car may be more efficient (and more fun to drive) but the sloppy saloon has just as much right to be on the road.

We are one nation, fat or thin. None of us should be blamed for 'costing' the nation more than anyone else, and experts should stop inventing numbers to make our flesh creep.

It puts them on the same level as the Fat Boy.

***

AFTER the retirement of its 96-year-old organist a village church in North Yorkshire replaced him … with a computer.

It is programmed to play pre-set accompaniments, without the help of a single human finger, to 150 popular hymns.

A musical curse upon this infernal machine!

May its synthetic sonorities be reduced to a tinkling cymbal!

May the mother of all viruses wipe every note from its memory, yea even to the uttermost quaver!

This contraption is neither musically nor spiritually equipped to do justice to the English hymn.

With a mere 150 in its reportoire, the computer is no match for Charles Wesley, who composed over 6000 hymns, still less for Julian's Dictionary of Hymnology (published in 1892), which lists nearly half a million.

St Augustine called hymns 'songs embodying the praise of God', and they have inspired great literary and musical effort.

Hymns Ancient And Modern — still the standard collection — includes poetry by Addison, Wordsworth, Tennyson, Bunyan and Milton, music by Parry, Stanford, Tallis, Sullivan and Handel, and a worthy host of lesser lights.

Even a Second Division team like HF Lyte and WH Monk can produce a Cup Final hymn: Abide With Me.

Such composers should not be reproduced mechanically as a form of holy Muzak. They deserve the interpretation of a human being with a soul.

Moreover, there are many churches where only a human organist can avert catastrophe.

When a hymn is composed in E Flat a computer knows only to play it in E Flat. It takes a real organist to recognize and react instantly when choir and congregation have elected to sing it in D Natural.

A real organist will also hold the opening chord of a hymn until *all* the congregation — even the village gossip — are ready to come in. He or she will pull out more stops to cover coughs and catarrhs, but throttle right down for the tiny choirboy's heartbreaking solo. These skills too are far beyond a computer.

At weddings, only a real organist knows how to cope when a bride or groom is AWOL. A quick glimpse at the anxious congregation, and the organist will 'vamp until ready', injecting a few extra bits of Bach or Buxtehude into the pre-match voluntary until the missing partner is located and put in the starting line-up.

In the same situation, a computer will plunge without thinking into the Mendelssohn Wedding March, drawing tactless attention to the absentee and provoking unnecessary tears and recriminations.

A real organist also proves his or her worth when a vicar's sermon goes on too long. When he has delivered 25 minutes on "Brotherly Love Among The Hittites And Hivites" with no signs of flagging the thoughtful organist will contrive to drop the hymn book onto the keyboard. No computer can deliver this warning. It will allow the vicar to bore straight through the Hivites and carry on to the Medes and the Persians.

It is amazing that the North Yorkshire village could not find a human replacement for the retiree. Where have all our organists gone? I blame karaoke.

In days gone by, you could find one under every bush. The Victorians had a hugely popular sentimental ballad, called The Volunteer Organist, about a shabby tramp who amazes a church congregation by his beautiful playing when their regular performer falls ill.

The village should scrap the computer and advertise for a musical tramp. Until they find one, they should go on bended knee and ask their 96-year-old to make a comeback.

It would be nice to think that he could 'vamp until ready' for another four years.

***

IT is some achievement to add more pollution to a Los Angeles atmosphere composed of car exhausts, sulphur, carbon monoxide, burning plastic, swimming-pool chemicals, flying bullets, personal fragrances, stale rumours, sun tan oil, over-heated television sets, dead fruit and rotting OJ Simpson merchandise, all mixed together by air conditioners.

But Los Angeles has indeed acquired a new and pervasive pollutant: the hamburger.

Environmental scientists have blamed the grilling of burgers and other fast food for releasing 33 tons of smoke and compounds *each day* into the soupy smog of the city, where people have begun to refer, without irony, to 'the oxygen layer'.

Apart from releasing noxious gases, burgers all too frequently generate other forms of pollution and damage. Thoughtlessly discarded packaging litters streets and clogs vital gutters. The mere sight of the average burger-slob eating one on the move — with surplus ketchup, relish and cheese oozing past slack lips onto chin(s) and clothing — is a form of visual blight.

On the subject of clothing, the scientists should investigate the close association between the eating of burgers and the wearing of polyester leisurewear, reversed baseball caps, or iridescent beach shorts (the latter should be made to carry a warning label: surfer gear does not suit a slacker body).

Burgers eaten in a moving car are a major source of damaged upholstery, damaged tempers of drivers and resultant damaged bodywork of adjacent vehicles.

The full horrors of the burger have landed on our country — an import as useless and fatal as the grey squirrel.

It has even pushed into our most cherished historic sites: Britain's railway stations.

For years the only food on offer in these places was a carbondated British Railways sandwich. In those vanished days, when Celia Johnson fell in love with Trevor Howard, a railway station smelt of trains — sooty, smoky, dieselly, oily, steamy, metallic, trains.

Now they all smell of burgers, bloody burgers. Our stations have acquired burger bars — all with cunningly designed extractor fans to remove the burger-gases from their customers and blow them over other passengers. Passive burgers are now as big a menace as passive smoking.

The only thing worse than passive burgers is passive popcorn in the cinema. After splitting themselves like amoebas into 'multiplexes' and thus forcing patrons to watch movies in a space no bigger than the average public lavatory, it is sheer cruelty by cinema-owners to fry their popcorn in remaindered engine oil which fills their tiny air-space with a monstrous, murky, mephitic miasma (which is terrible for my as'ma and anyone else's...)

However, it is only fair to say that fast food may have saved the Earth. The gases it emits could be detected in our atmosphere by enemy aliens through spectral analysis. They would be a major deterrent to invasion.

The Mekon or Darth Vader would demand an explanation from his Chief Scientist for the mysterious lines on his screen. "It can only mean one thing, Your Mightiness. The Earthlings eat hamburgers and popcorn."

"Curses! Divert the space fleet to Jupiter! At least we'll be able to breathe..."

***

FEW people should be surprised that Church of England clergy are flocking to join the trade union MSF.

It is, after all, a union for white-collar workers, although one does feel that it should change its name to accommodate its latest band of brothers and sisters. Clergy cannot be classed as Manufacturing, nor Science, and they certainly do not belong under Finance, remembering what Jesus thought of those nice money-changers in the Temple...

If MSF continues to recruit members to its new clerical section it might choose to call itself simply the Divine Workers Union. This could give it a valuable negotiating weapon: few other unions could threaten employers with a plague of locusts for failing to concede their demands.

As a hardworking, poorly paid section of labour, with growing worries about job security, Anglican clergy are well-advised to get a union behind them. They can cite much Biblical authority behind the basic principles of trade unionism. Ecclesiastes 4 offers a ringing endorsement of collective action: "Two are better than one: because they have a good reward for their labour. Woe to him that is alone when he falleth for he hath not another to help him up".

However, other texts might require some judicious editing. Few union bargainers would be happy with Matthew 20 and the parable of the labourers in the vineyard. A penny all round, with no differentials for skills or anti-social hours... brothers and sisters, that offer from management is an insult.

Even the Ten Commandments sit uneasily with some of the demands of modern trade unionism.

Again some slight revisions might be expedient. "Forty hours shalt thou labour and do thy work, with a target of thirty-five hours as soon as economic conditions allow."

"Thou shalt not covet thy neighbour's house ... but thou shalt definitely covet his wages."

If trade unionism does take root within the Church of England it could make dramatic changes in its doctrine and practices.

The Church so far has relied on just Thirty-Nine Articles. This is far too few for a trade union rule book and it will have to go up to at least 153.

Hymn boards would acquire a new use to announce the results of card votes.

After the recent spate of well-publicized conversions to Roman Catholicism, the Church might well seek to protect its membership by a 'no-poaching' agreement for souls.

One dreads to imagine what would happen if the newly-unionized clergy actually became involved in an industrial dispute.

A go-slow by vicars could return us to the days of four-hour sermons. If they actually came out on strike, would flying pickets be replaced by flying pulpits? Would we hear announcements like those of British Rail? "The following services will be running today: the 6-30 Evensong from St Cuthbert's in Upson Downs..." And when the strike was finally settled would vicars work double time to clear the backlog? If so, Four Weddings And A Funeral could be over before Wet Wet Wet had even felt it in their toes.

Although all these difficulties may lie ahead I feel sure that more and more clergy will see the benefits of union member-ship.

They can certainly take inspiration from the union which was founded some years ago by a local woodworker. In spite of early betrayals and persecutions it now has branches in every part of the world and offers an astonishing range of benefits to its members.

***

NOT for the first time in its history, Burgundy has become a battlefield.

A war as fierce as it is absurd has broken out in the world of wine. The armies involved are wine critics. On one side are the Old Guard, or premiers crus, mostly British, with strong links to the wine trade. They favour sonorous abstractions to describe wine, using such terms as 'vigour', 'vitality' or 'harmony'.

On the other side are the critics nouveaux, mostly American, self-consciously irreverent and iconoclastic. They have enraged the premiers crus with a display of flashy metaphors and similes. To them a wine may smell or even taste like 'hamster cages', or 'cream of mushroom soup', or 'horse manure' (as a compliment) or even 'wet dog'.

They have enlisted science on their side, using gas chromatography to detect the presence of asparagus in the bouquet of a white Sauvignon. (Yes, but can they find melted butter in a Vouvray?)

The nouveaux are clearly winning the war. In more and more restaurants the wine-list has turned into a recipe book: "this popular Albanian Riesling has honey, oregano, violet and spring lamb in its make-up, with an aftermath of gooseberry."

This must be resisted. No one should need a doctorate in chemistry to understand a wine list, nor a course in contem-porary literary criticism to 'de-construct' it. When I order a bottle of Red Infuriator I do not expect to become a Post-Modernist but a Pissed-Modernist.

However, defeat of the new army should not lead to a restoration of the ancien régime. The old critics must take some responsibility for the shibboleths, rituals and unnecessary protocols which for so many years ruined wine for the British.

Our country does not grow much wine but we are still the world's leading producer of wine snobs. We export them, like our nannies, to teach other countries how to behave: which wines to serve with what and at which temperatures, which glasses to use, even how to open a bottle and rotate it around a table.

Wine-producer countries treat it as a friend to be greeted, not a monarch to be crowned. The episcopal wine waiter, who uses flummery and ceremony to indicate his disdain for the customer, is a peculiarly British pest. (The following exchange may be usefully employed to put such a character in his place. "Wine waiter, do you have a white Macon?" "Yes." "Well, take it off, it isn't raining.")

It is time for us peasants to stage a mass uprising against all wine critics, anciens or nouveaux. We do not need florid metaphors or empty sonorities to tell us what to drink. There have never been more countries producing wine: one can travel the world in one's off-licence. We should take a year of wine-hopping, flitting from vineyard to vineyard, changing faster than traffic lights between red, white and rosé, to discover what we enjoy.

Let us trample all the rules like grapes beneath our feet, silence all critics and sentence all wine snobs to Gourmet Night at Fawlty Towers. Then we shall be free to follow the poetic advice of Edmund Spenser: "pour out the wine without restraint or stay, pour not by cups but by the bellyful".

***

THE MINISTRY of Defence, of all people, have just done something remarkably creative.

It could provide the cheapest but most effective form of defence which our nation has ever enjoyed. It could even raise our quality of life to heights never before attempted, let alone achieved.

The men from the ministry have just sold a disused US Air Force Base in Suffolk to the Natural Law Party, the followers of the Maharishi Mahesh Yogi. Apart from recruiting George Harrison and losing election deposits, they are best known for their belief in 'yogic flying', which uses meditation techniques to make the body hover and manoeuvre in mid-air.

The Anglian skies, once filled with the hum of American bombers, will now echo to the 'Om' of transcendental pilots.

It would be an excellent idea if they could take over the air defence of these islands.

A squadron of yogic flyers, deflecting evil intruders by the power of thought, would be a cheap and reliable alternative to a squadron of computer systems packed in energy-guzzling heavier-than-air machines. We could cancel the new Euro-fighter (or sell it to Eurodisney, which needs a new attraction).

The yogic squadron would of course have to undergo a test flight. An early experiment in meditational defence was not very promising. At the height of American protests against the Vietnam war, one group attempted to enchant the Pentagon and lift it off the ground. However the building and its employees stayed very firmly put (the enchanters needed more powerful thought-waves and no one then had the wit to send for Forrest Gump).

Apart from defence, yogic flying offers great possibilities for public transport. Commuters could hover and glide to their destinations in comfort (and junior ministers would not have to share any air space with dreadful human beings). In health and education yogic flying could ease acute problems of space without the need for expensive new beds, wards and classrooms.

In Parliament the technique would help Madam Speaker, Betty Boothroyd, to discipline unruly or insulting MPs. "I suspend the honourable member" would mean what it says: an offending MP could be made to hover in mid-air over his colleagues until she thought he had learnt his lesson.

Indeed almost every area of our national life could benefit from yogic flying (although it might be unwise to teach it to prisoners, since enough of them are escaping by conventional means).

In sport, yogic flying might have help our cricketers to catch something more than a cold in a Test Match. In football, centre forwards could literally 'hang in the air', their ankles safe from earthbound defending choppers.

Every imaginative act attracts carpers and critics, and a Labour MP has protested to the Armed Forces Minister, Nicholas Soames, against the sale of the air base to the Natural Law Party.

Mr Soames should ignore him. He should think what his grandfather, Winston Churchill might have said: Law-Law is better than War-War.

***

A TERRIFYING report threatens to remove all the pleasure from drinking tea. The American Health Foundation has announced that it is good for you. It claims that five cups will match the nutrition offered by half a day's intake of fresh vegetables. It will also fight cancer strokes and heart disease.

The claim deserves a squeeze of scepticism. If tea really were that wonderful Britain's civil servants would be the healthiest people in the world. And Bristow the buying clerk slave to the trolley at the giant Chester-Perry organization, would be Mr Universe.

There is of course a catch in the Foundation's report. It expects tea to be taken in the American style. Without milk.

Is there a sinister political agenda? Does the Foundation really care about health or is it making propaganda for the American way of life?

But for once the Americans have right on their side.

Putting milk in tea is one of history's great errors, on a par with Marxism, karaoke and the internal combustion engine.

When tea first caught on in Britain under Charles II it was invariably served black or green. Milk crept in during the eighteenth century, an unscrupulous invention by Georgian marketing men to help eliminate a dairy surplus.

Nature fashioned tea as a perfect infusion. If any additive is required it should be a piece of lemon, or better still lime. If one is going to add milk, why not throw in a nourishing slab of yak butter like the Tibetans?

Notwithstanding the Milk Heresy, our history bears witness to the vital influence of tea. Wellington took tea with him on all his campaigns. Napoleon, hit by the English blockade, had to rely on ersatz substitutes. This, rather than the late arrival of the Prussians, is the real reason why Waterloo Station is in London instead of Paris.

British armies have fought on tea for centuries. As each generation of soldiers has discovered, there is Something In It which depresses their libido and makes them concentrate all their energies on their fighting tasks. Hundreds of enemy agents have perished in the effort to discover the secret Naafi formula. By concentrating only on the nutritional properties of tea, the American Health Foundation lost sight of its social and psychological benefits.

The health-giving properties of tea are multiplied a thousand-fold if it is taken as a tea break. This relieves stress and encourages conversation and creativity. No sensible business should allow its employees to drink tea at their place of work. They should be made to travel at least as far as a tea trolley, better still a canteen. A really enlightened business would offer tea dances for its employees and encourage them to glide with each other as a live Orphean orchestra plays selections from Rodgers and Hart.

Such a move would revive the association of tea with luxury and romance and deliver it from the tyranny of the health fanatics. Like all great pleasures tea should feel illicit and dangerous, not drab and nutritious. Tea is far too good to be left to the goody-goodies.

***

IN A NIGHTMARE marriage of voodoo science and health fascism, genetic engineers in California have come up with a process to take caffeine out of the cells of coffee plants.

Coffee without caffeine. It's like Wise without Morecambe, or Garfunkel without Simon. It's like Dracula with dentures. It's a cinema showing nothing but Shirley Temple. It's like the Chippendales in white tie and tails. It's An Evening With Nigel Mansell.

What is the point of coffee without the magic elixir at its heart? As Cole Porter might have said: "It's de-lightful, it's de-licious, it's de-caffeinated... and it's de-reary!"

Some people like that kind of coffee. Some favour it for medical reasons. Very well, they can have it. There will never be a shortage of decaffeinated coffee. It is a simple chemical process to remove caffeine from coffee beans or grounds by solvents.

But now the caffeinophobes will be able to inflict their in-sipid tastes on all the rest of us. What other motive could there be for taking caffeine out of the original *plant?* A biologi-cal nanny is descending on the world — a threat to liberty and intellect alike.

Coffee — with caffeine — has always been associated with free thinking and creativity. Tyrants and fanatics have regularly tried to ban it. It is no coincidence that the coffee-houses of the seventeenth century were the birthplace of Britain's independent newspapers. The American and French Revolutions were fuelled by coffee.

Coffee conquered the world precisely because it acts not only on the senses but on the mind — through caffeine.

That is why it earned this tribute from Talleyrand, the great French diplomat: "Suave molecules of Mocha stir up your blood without causing excessive heat, the organ of thought receives from it a feeling of sympathy: work becomes easier."

Talleyrand lived to be over eighty. During his career he out-witted Napoleon *and* Wellington. Despite physical and spiritual handicaps he made love to many beautiful women. His grandson was another French Foreign Minister, and he might well have fathered the painter Delacroix. Could he have done any of this on decaffeinated? Could he cocoa!

There is a long list of legendary coffee drinkers. Bach com-posed a cantata in its honour. Dr Johnson said some of his greatest lines over coffee — real coffee. On decaffeinated he would probably have become a chat show host, like Boswell.

And where would today's greatest hero be without his regular pot of strong coffee — Garfield the Cat? On decaffeinated he would just be a *pet*.

Kingsley Amis once created the perfect beer commercial: So-And-So's Beer Makes You Drunk! In imitation I offer: So-And-So's Coffee Makes You Jump!

Coffee is stimulating, exciting and dangerous. It was meant to be that way: Nature put a drug into it. For that reason, real coffee drinkers of any age can consider themselves adults — people trusted to take responsibility for their bodies and minds.

Breeding coffee plants without caffeine is another step towards a world in which *everything* has to be safe for children — not only food and drink, but thought.

***

AT FIRST it sounded macabre, but on second thoughts some people in Tewkesbury, Gloucestershire, should be congratulated for a charming and thoughtful gesture.

They invited one of their friends, a 92-year-old church warden, to celebrate his life by attending his own memorial service.

I have never seen the logic of the old maxim 'de mortuis nil nisi bonum'. If people have anything good to say about me, I would like to hear it when I am alive, and when I can use it in support of a pay claim. When I am gone they can rubbish me as much as they like.

Memorial services for the living (perhaps in this context one might call them 'the pre-deceased') offer other advantages. As Reggie Perrin discovered on television many years ago, they give the subject a check on the number and demeanour of the mourners.

More important, they give him or her some control over the eulogy. Indeed, the pre-deceased would be well advised to compose this themselves, if not actually deliver it. That way they can be sure that all of their achievements will be recorded, including many which may not have come to the attention of family or friends.

In my own case, I would like my mourners to have full details of my unpublicized work as an adviser to the judges of the Nobel Prize for Literature and of my corrections to the manuscript of Professor Stephen Hawking's Brief History Of Time. I would also like to take them through my hat-trick for the Upper Fifth against the Lower Fourth and to deny the story of my subsequent visit to the school tuck-shop with the umpire.

It is no easy task to compose one's own eulogy. Glenda Jackson, Ken Russell, and Spike Milligan discovered this some years ago on the Channel Four television series, The Obituary Show. More recently, Sir Jimmy Savile's was so convincing that Radio One disc jockey Chris Morris believed him to be actually dead, a mistake corrected by libel lawyers.

My greatest problems have been in editing. Even after savage cuts, my eulogy is already the length of David Copperfield, and I expect to be spared for quite a few more years. I have therefore decided that it would be fairer to incorporate it into my will: only those who expect something from my estate will be forced to listen to the chapters on I Am Born... I Observe... I Have A Change...

A will is in fact an excellent way of being published. One can say what one likes in a will so long as it is not defamatory (dead men cannot sue but they can be sued) knowing that it will eventually be read out and made public. Conventional publishers are becoming more and more reluctant to bring out new writers unless they are celebrities: publication by will could soon be the only hope for anyone else. Eventually we might even have a Booker Prize for the Posthumous.

Meanwhile I hope that Tewkesbury's gesture is copied elsewhere. A memorial service is often described as a service of thanksgiving, and a thank-you means so much more when the recipient can hear it.

Who Will Buy?
(From *The Shop Of Little Horrors*)

POWERFUL commercial interests have killed off a brave campaign to extend consumer protection to one of America's most helpless minorities. Men.

A bill which would have banned them from shopping malls has died in the Florida legislature. Its sponsor, Everett Kelly, said that men in malls were driven off their trolley by the experience. Only women were strong enough to survive it, let alone enjoy it. His proposal would have allowed men only into sport shops, boat shows and hardware stores.

Even critics of his sexism can admire Mr Kelly's chivalry. A shopping mall is not for the weak, of either sex. It is, truly, a brave new world, of strange magic and artificial delights.

If Shakespeare were writing 'The Tempest' today he would set it not in Bermuda but a shopping mall. Indeed, quite uncannily, he predicted the mall's piped music and air conditioning when he made Caliban say "The aisle is full of noises, sounds and sweet airs that give delight and hurt not. Sometimes a thousand twangling instruments will hum about mine ears, and sometimes voices that, if I had then waked after long sleep will make me shop again..."

To be in a shopping mall is to crash-land on an alien planet. It has no familiar sun, and therefore no east and west, but is bathed instead in the filtered, sinister light of some strange, dwarfish star. Its manufactured plants and water-falls are a mocking reminder of a far-distant Earth.

Once on the surface, cut off from escape by car or public transport, the lost traveller quickly discovers the law of Planet Mall: you will shop.

Other activities are barely tolerated, some actively persecuted. Any food or drink served in a mall will be fast and expensive (but child-appealing). Every mouthful says "Finish me quickly, and get back to your shopping". Toilets will be remote and barely visible, and impatient queues will discourage lingering.

A mall offers almost nowhere for a normal-size adult to sit down without making a purchase. Its benches are ergophobically designed to discomfit any known size and shape of bottom. Only a trained, professional slacker will find it possible to lounge in a shopping mall, which is why these places are so popular with teenagers.

Anyone who, by miracle, achieves sleep in a mall is ejected by security personnel as a subversive. Very soon the same treatment will be applied to newspaper readers.

A mall expects you not only to shop but to do a lot of shopping in different places. Its shops are distributed randomly and illogically, so that no one can complete a shopping list without making a zigzagging, floor-hopping circuit of the premises.

For the same reason, maps in a shopping mall are deliberately few and vague, to minimize the risk that shoppers might find what they actually want to buy. Mall designers know that a shopper in perpetual motion is more likely to make an impulsive purchase. That accounts for the number of businesses in shopping malls which sell goods and services you would never dream of buying anywhere else: things like magnetic window cleaners, or histories of your family name which prove that you ought to be on the throne instead of the Queen.

Although it is sad that Mr Kelly's bill was defeated, hope is at hand for the victims of Stressed Shopping Syndrome (or mall de mer as it is sometimes known).

It is called home shopping and it allows Mr Kelly's good ol' boys to ogle sports goods, boats and hardware without leaving their beer and their television set.

***

SETTING a new milestone in animal protection, a pet shop owner in Cardiff is to charge children a £1 fee for entering his premises because they cause stress to his reptiles.

This is a sad but necessary deterrent. Quite rightly, most children love reptiles and cannot wait to see them. If a reptile is not on view, the average child will, in 0.3 of a nano-second, tap on the glass of its home to make it come out.

Glass-tappers are a nightmare to any reptile or indeed amphibian, insect or mollusc. In human terms, it is the equivalent of being made to rise from a siesta to answer the door for a double-glazing salesman. Imagine that happening to you, all day long.

If the Cardiff proprietor teaches children to show patience with reptiles he will have performed a great service for both species.

With proper care, reptiles can be the perfect family pet. They are beautiful, space-saving, sociable (when awake), and have interesting feeding habits. Many will provide an attractive collector's item by shedding their skin. A gregarious garter snake is a far better gift for Mother's Day than conventional flowers or chocolates or a badly-made breakfast in bed.

The idea of an entrance fee will appeal to other retailers beyond the pet trade, in recognition of the appalling stress which customers can cause.

I am well aware of my own limitations as a customer. I am often begged to leave fashionable clothing stores by tearful assistants, but why *shouldn't* I wear flares?

My reputation as a gardener has preceded me. When I enter a flower shop, I can sense terrified azaleas cowering in their pots, whispering "Please, not me?" Such shops have a right to protect themselves against me as the customer from Hell. However, I should have a parallel right to defend myself as a homeowner and homeworker against door-to-door and telephone salespeople.

After taking legal advice I have amended the notice by my doorbell. It used to read "I Do Not Buy Anything From My Door. That Includes Salvation."

I have now added the words "If You Still Wish Me To Listen To Your Sales Talk, I Will Charge You At The Rate Of £10 Per Minute. Ringing My Bell Constitutes Acceptance Of A Contract."

For tele-hucksters, I have a compendious answerphone

message. "If you are making a six-figure offer for my novel and/or screenplay, please touch One. If this is a social call, please touch Two. If I owe you money and the cheque in the post has not yet arrived, please touch Three. I do not want a free inspection of my windows when you are in my neighbourhood, nor a free demonstration of your carpet-cleaner.

"If after touching One or Two you attempt to sell me anything at all you will receive a visit — from me *and* my snake."

***

A BOLD initiative by Trafford Council in Cheshire could revolutionize local government finance.

It has decided to charge local supermarkets £25 for the return of lost or abandoned trolleys.

This source of revenue has been staring councils in the face. Sad trolleys congregating to die in an elephants' graveyard of decaying metal are an everyday feature of the British street scene.

If Trafford is anything like my local neighbourhood it should make enough from its new trolley tax to build a new town hall. If receipts proved to be sluggish the council could infiltrate its own employees into local supermarkets just before closing time to smuggle trolleys into the surrounding streets.

The beauty of the scheme is that supermarkets would have to pay up. Without trolleys, their profits would collapse and the economy of the Western world would go into a tailspin.

In 'Meet Me In St Louis' Judy Garland performed a delightful number called The Trolley Song. Today she would do it in a supermarket and the chorus would run "Slide, slide, slide went the trolley. Ring, ring, ring, went the till. Zing, zing, zing went my heartstrings When the check-out presented my bill."

The supermarket trolley has turned every shopping trip into a voyage of discovery.

Before the trolley — amazing as it seems — people went to a shop or market with a list and a basket and were supplied with the things they wanted from an assistant.

But the trolley makes shoppers float aimlessly through a sea of merchandise. It induces relaxation, even a mild form of hypnosis. Lists are forgotten; entranced shoppers are tempted by new luxuries: as another old song might have put it "Pack up your truffles in your plastic bag and smile, smile, smile…"

For this reason, a wise supermarket will fit a speed control to its trolleys. The unscrupulous may even have them magnetized, so that customers are pulled away from boring (and low-profit) shelves of washing powder and attracted instead to special displays of (high-value) organic cocktail snacks.

The really unscrupulous, when business is slack, will employ actors as make-believe customers.

This secret practice explains the person who always seems to be in front of you in the check-out queue — the cantankerous complainer trying to buy two tins of baked beans with out-of-date special offer coupons. He or she is there simply to induce you to put some more items in your trolley in a frenzy of boredom.

Supermarkets may well attempt counter-measures against a trolley tax. Some might try electronic tagging, to make their trolleys scream every time they were pushed beyond the perimeter of the car park. Others might employ special SAS search-and-seize teams to repossess their trolleys before the council could get them.

But supermarkets could easily recoup the trolley tax by making customers pass a driving test. The examiner might say "I am going to ask you to pull in at the next butter counter and make a three-point turn finishing in front of the rhubarb yoghurt. From there I will ask you to change lanes safely and with the appropriate hand-signal for coleslaw. Later you will make an emergency stop as if you had suddenly remembered the cat food."

In this way, the trolley tax could improve safety besides raising revenue and improving the environment.

But before introducing one, local councils should ask themselves a simple question. Do they conduct their business with the same efficiency and care for customers as their local supermarkets?

***

THE MOST pointless invention of the year, the decade, and even the millenium, must be the bank cash dispenser which plays canned background music to customers.

Using these things in public is already an embarrassing experience, and often a dangerous one.

You can almost sense the machine talking over your shoulder to the people behind you in the queue. "I'm not giving *him* £90 — he hasn't got the price of a cup of tea... Wrong PIN number. Absent-minded twit. Or maybe it isn't his card at all. Anyone want to phone the police?... Ooh, look at Mr Flash, taking out £200 in notes. Why not mug him before he can get to his car?"

When you ask for your current balance the machine immediately offers to flash the result on the screen for all to see. Why stop there? Why not put it up in lights over Piccadilly Circus?

The banks could even invite customers to guess the size of their overdrafts when they interrogate the machine, as in The Price Is Right. The people in the queue could join in the fun with shouts of "Higher! Higher!"

Cash dispenser misery can only be deepened by the accompaniment of music. Imagine being greeted, on seeking a cash withdrawal, by the strains of "Hey, Big Spender!" Or receiving your current balance to the Dead March in Saul.

The awful device has been invented by the Muzak company, who have already driven millions of people to stagger upstairs rather than enter a lift. They say that it can also carry advertising. The average transaction time of thirty seconds is apparently enough to deliver a quick-hitting, succinct message.

Cash dispensers could be especially attractive to advertisers because their customers are totally trapped. They cannot skip the commercial to make a cup of tea, visit the lavatory or attend to a cat. They have to watch or listen to it before they get any cash.

The only advertising which could possibly interest me on a bank cash dispenser screen would be for cheap air tickets to Brazil. One-way.

Teaching cash dispensers to play music and deliver advertising is only the first step on a path to nightmare. Inevitably, someone will give them an 'eye' to look at their customers. They could spot whether they were accompanied by a child, and instantly flash up an advertisement for an expensive toy.

Worst of all, a cash dispenser might be given enough of a 'mind' to hold a real conversation.

It could quickly become a nag and a tyrant. "Ah! We meet again, number 2834. Don't bother to change your PIN number. I'll always know it's you. Don't pretend you want a statement. You only love me for my money…"

But even worse, an 'intelligent machine' might start to take pity on its customers.

Imagine going to the cash dispenser on a Friday evening and asking for a £20 withdrawal. Instead of delivering the dosh, the machine flashes or even speaks a message of sympathy "Only £20 for the whole weekend? No plans? Staying at home with the TV and a pizza? Poor baby. Why don't I give you £80 and you can ask someone for a date? Or why not buy some better clothes? The Oxfam shop is open in the High Street until 5 tomorrow."

If the banks really wanted to do something for their customers they would ignore Muzak's infernal invention. People do not want music or commercials with their money — but thousands would flock to the first bank which combined its cash dispensers with a mini-bar.

***

WHERE else but California would a psycho-therapist offer to treat people with an irrational fear of shopping?

Dr Gilly of Los Angeles gives counselling sessions which take victims by gentle stages from theft local candy store until they are ready for the ultimate challenge of a mall. Her greatest success story has just booked himself a month's vacation at Harrods.

Fear of shopping, or *emptophobia* to give it a scientific name, has only recently been recognized as a distinct disorder.

Many still confuse it with chrematophobia, the fear of touching money.

Victims of this condition can frequently be found in licensed premises. They appear totally normal, even sociable, in company for several rounds. But when it is suggested that they may have to use money to purchase further drinks, chrematophobia takes hold.

They show extreme stress, and the typical victim will demonstrate a compulsive need to look at his watch while inventing fantasies of urgent appointments elsewhere. The worst sufferers never take the risk of carrying money on their person, but milder cases have been known to offer to pay with a £50 note bearing the likeness of King George VI.

Emptophobes have no problems with money. It is shopping they cannot stand.

Their condition is allied to batophobia (the fear of high buildings), decidophobia (decisions), and macrophobia (long waits) — but most closely of all to katagelophobia (fear of ridicule).

Shopping anywhere, anyhow, for any thing brings a constant risk of misery and humiliation.

Even the simplest basic purchases are a hazardous undertaking. Take for example a visit to the corner shop for a daily newspaper. Unwary shoppers often do this in sloppy clothes without the benefit of shaving or make-up. This simply invites the shopkeeper (and other customers) to look up at the time in a marked manner, as if to say "Just got out of bed, have we? No job to go to?"

Even more social dangers lurk at the supermarket — starting with the parking lot, superbly designed to demonstrate any lack of parking skills to a honking queue of other drivers.

Once inside, there is the sneering band of healthy eaters who dine the routes to the junk food counter.

Then comes the nerve-wracking inspection of the shopper's

purchases by the check-out clerk, who will display to other customers any item which is especially cheap or past its sell-by date.

Worse still is buying clothes, which forces the shopper to reveal his or her current wardrobe to an astonished and often giggling assistant.

When I decide (about every five years) to buy a good suit I can only do it in stages — changing store by store into a series of progressively better suits. I begin by sneaking into a charity store, then I move to a low-budget multiple, then to somewhere with an Italian name... Only in this final outfit will I dare enter the tailor of my choice. I have the same problem with shoes and coats. My closets are full of intermediate garments — worn only once.

Dr Gilly may be able to help victims of clothing stores. But some shopping missions are beyond therapy. If one is mechanically ignorant, nothing can overcome the embarrassment of buying a spare part for a motor car.

On The Sheet Where You Live...

IN A VAIN pursuit of progress and politesse, the county of South Yorkshire sent its dustmen to charm school.

People first went to charm school to become air hostesses or Joan Collins. It is a mark of social and sexual revolution if these places are now teaching deportment to dustmen. They will no doubt learn to balance bins on their heads, to model a range of dustwear and accessories, to crook their little fingers before drinking a mug of tea (and to remove the spoon first), and after graduation to call themselves 'recycling engineers'.

South Yorkshire's investment is totally misguided. Charm has nothing to add to the role of a dustman. He should be a strong, silent type: a Gary Cooper rather than a Cary Grant — and certainly not a Hugh Grant.

A good dustman is a lonely Mr Clean in a dirty world. He patrols the sleeping streets at dawn — and he should let them remain the sleeping streets at dawn. He should not engage their inhabitants in witty conversations, or provide them with sparkling film reviews or unique insights into contemporary politics.

If I want any of that I can always get into a taxi.

My dustman and I meet on my doorstep once a year. We do not trade views on Postmodernism. He says "Dustman." I fight down an impulse to say "I've already got one." Instead I draw his attention to an envelope labelled 'Dustman'. We both say "Merry Christmas!" The exchange may lack charm but it is simple and eloquent and is used by many other households.

Charm school could all too easily tempt the South Yorkshire dustmen to talk like American waiters. Bleary-eyed Barnsleyites will not enjoy being woken to "Hi! I'm John. I'll be your bin man for this morning. I see from your refuse that your special last night was a takeaway pizza from

Luigi's. For tonight's special may I recommend the chicken tikka masala from Gandhi's? And if you don't believe me, ask your neighbours at Number 27!"

Rather than charm, dustmen should be given a firm grounding in the practical skills of their calling. These should include lid technique. "Do not use the lid as a frisbee. Instead, take the handle of the lid in either your right or your left hand. Raise it with the handle pointing towards the sky. Keeping this position, lower it gently over the bin in such a way as to exclude rainwater."

Following logically from that lesson would be a course in biology. "If the customer has allowed rainwater to accumulate in a bin or bin lid, do not pour the resulting stagnant festering liquid over his azalea. The shock will be too great. Only a geranium can stand this treatment. If you cannot find one, tip the stuff into the gutter."

Charm is a much over-rated virtue in English life, and not just for dustmen. The English still prefer Charles II, the Merrie Monarch, to stern Oliver Cromwell, but who was the better ruler? Throughout our history charm has given a protective coating to spies, confidence tricksters and politicians. Charm today produces diplomats who are superb with cocktails and canapes but not so good over beef.

We should let our dustmen be dustmen. They do a vital and thankless job. We should be grateful if they do it competently and not try to turn them into Fred Astaire.

***

NINETEEN years after it was first mailed, the German postal service finally succeeded in delivering a parcel to its addressee, Herr Hermann Nagel of Goslar. The contents — a priceless antique wine glass — arrived in perfect condition. But after opening the parcel an over-excited Herr Nagel dropped the glass on his doorstep, where it shattered into fragments.

In my view, the entire blame for this tragedy lies with the postal service. Anyone with minimal foresight could have

63

anticipated the result of delivering a long-lost fragile object to a clearly besotted connoisseur.

Herr Nagel should have been invited to open the parcel in a specially-padded room. As recompense for the delay, the post office should also have presented him with a case of vintage wine from 1977 — the year in which the glass should have arrived.

The Germans' thoughtless behaviour is typical of postal services throughout the world.

They deliver absolutely anything through a letter box, just because it has been addressed to somebody, with no consideration for its effect on the recipient.

Day after day, innocent people are driven to misery or terror by letters from their banks, their landlords or property managers, their creditors, their local authority or a government department. For these people, a postal strike is not an inconvenience but a truce...

A well-organized Post Office would not deliver such items without warning. Instead it would leave a note, similar to those used when it is unable to deliver a bulky parcel.

"You have been sent a letter from the Inland Revenue. It contains red print. Please indicate a time when you will feel strong enough to receive it. Alternatively you may wish to collect it from our *licensed* depot, where stimulants and revivers are available during normal opening hours."

An ideal Post Office would allow people to opt out of such letters altogether, as they can already apply to be taken off the list for junk mail. However, this would probably induce the Inland Revenue to disguise its Final Demands as personal mail.

For example, it might have them delivered as holiday postcards from Majorca. "Very hot. Kids having great time in pool but Dad passed out from sangria on welcome evening you owe us £823-26 ha-ha gotcha!"

Such subterfuges might make people terrified of receiving any post whatsoever. In that case the Post Office should provide the ultimate service, of pre-reading people's mail before delivery.

The postie would then be able to recite the highlights to the recipient and provide an appropriate response (in my case, almost invariably sympathy).

"Your car won't be ready for three weeks, diabolical, but next time why don't you let my brother-in-law have a look at it? They've rejected your movie script, shame, I thought it was great but why don't you change the extra-terrestrial into a dinosaur? I had exactly the same trouble with my roof, in the end had to have a new one. Your girl friend still doesn't want to see you ... but there's lots of other pebbles on the beach..."

This kind of human touch may soon be the only way in which traditional mail can compete with the ruthless automata of e-mail and fax.

And if any day's delivery proved completely unbearable, a caring postie would provide the only possible comfort.

Reciting the misfortunes of the neighbours.

***

IN 1960 a bad shave cost Richard Nixon the Presidency of the United States. In his first televised debate with John F Kennedy voters only had eyes for his stubbly jowls. They confirmed his image as 'Tricky Dicky', the shifty salesman (as in, would you buy a used country from this man?)

If Nixon could have run against me, he would have won by a landslide. He had five o'clock shadow: I have darkness at noon. But now I hope for a smoother passage. Mr Gary of Trumper's, the gentlemen's hairdressers, has taught me to shave. No more rashes, no more cuts: his one-hour lesson has released me from thirty-two years in the nick.

Rule number one: get up early. A proper shave, says Mr Gary, should last at least ten minutes (adolescents will need that much time simply to find any facial follicle to remove) and be preceded by a bath or shower as a preliminary warning to the skin. While the mirror demists, he recommends a pause for the pores under a hot lime-scented towel.

I have never owned a badger-hair shaving brush, partly because I am an animal-lover but largely because I am a cheapskate. But there is still no better way of applying shaving cream (rose-scented), which should be achieved in a light, circular motion. This can be done clockwise or anti-clockwise, but not in opposition to the Earth's magnetic field.

A little finger massage of the cream, then plunge into the hottest possible water the safety razor of your choice. Most faces welcome one of those double-bladed numbers with that lubricating widget on top.

You are now ready, like a skier, for that first glorious downhill run along the virgin stubble, all the way from the sideburn to the uppermost chin, with a slalom turn at the jaw.

All shaving should be downhill, says Mr Gary, although he will allow for a little sideslipping along the moustache. Long, calm strokes are best, and for that reason great care must be taken in the choice of background radio. No one should ever shave to the news or the Today programme, which are likely to provoke outrage, but the shipping forecast is ideal: its exotic names, Malin, Rockall, Bailey, South-East Iceland, provide a soothing mantra to accompany the razor.

For obvious reasons, all shaving should be done *before* opening any letter from the Inland Revenue or a bookmaker. A shaver should ignore savagely any request to answer a telephone, find games kit or feed a pet.

Inspection by mirror should be supplemented with the fingertips. If you want to grow a goatee on your own head be it, but there is no point in leaving stubble accidentally. When satisfied that you have removed all you wish, you may rinse and then dab, never rub, dry. A natural aftershave, or better, skin food gives the face its final treat, and no gentleman should be too embarrassed to use a moisturizer last thing at night.

Mr Gary recommends not shaving at weekends. This would give valuable extra time to read your favourite quality Sunday newspaper, but may run into opposition from loved ones.

A great shave involves trouble and expense, but it is still the cheapest way known to man to feel like a million dollars. And it would be worth two million dollars to learn how to get one in a shared family bathroom.

ONE of the world's great love affairs has ended in tears.

The British people have turned against their waffle-maker. A survey by Which? magazine found it the least popular device in British households. As many as 86 per cent regretted that they had ever bought one.

It marks the end of an era. It seems only yesterday that Britain sizzled with merry waffle parties. Flared couples bopped and boogied around the grill to the beat of Abba's monster hit Waffleloo.

But now the mighty machine which made it all happen sits forgotten in the back of the kitchen cupboard, guarded by crusted sentinels of maple syrup. Only our politicians keep alive the art of British waffle.

The survey found similar levels of disenchantment with yoghurt makers and tea makers. This is hardly surprising. A yoghurt maker is not a convenience: it is a life sentence — to yoghurt. Its very presence in a kitchen sends out a subliminal message: "Make some yoghurt. You like yoghurt. Why did you pay money for me if you don't like yoghurt? I saw you with that orange sorbet last night. Don't you love me any more?"

The tea maker is a gigantic confidence trick. Billed as a device to wake you up, it simply encourages you to stay in bed. On a rough morning, it is not tea which wakes you up but the craving for tea, a force which pulls you onto your feet and into the kitchen, where you discover the will to perform other tasks, such as feeding the cats or finding the toy in the children's cereal.

The Which? survey might have had a different result if it had included the mobile phone — another confidence trick. Far from being mobile, most of these oblige the user to remain static, in a tortured position (usually leaning from a car window at a 315-degree angle over the hard shoulder), to pick up a signal weaker than those transmitted by the Pioneer spacecraft beyond the planet Neptune.

Which? should also have explored attitudes to DIY furniture, which has brought untold frustration and fury to its purchasers. This can be ascribed entirely to the accompanying instructions, which are full of gobbledegook like "slide the Grommet (B) into the Wallace slot (Q)."

It is a little-known fact that all assembly instructions for DIY furniture are translated from the original Albanian. By a machine.

Which? also missed out several exotic but tempting gadgets which are regularly offered by mail. One is that curious fetishistic device which measures the heights of ceilings, which is supplied (under plain cover) to people with secret fantasies of being an estate agent.

Then there is Fido the Magic Dog, who gives a weather forecast. Just put him outdoors: if he turns wet it must be raining. There are those energy-pyramids which claim to revive dead plants and razor bladers. If pyramids are such wonderful revivers, why don't we see the Pharaohs having disco nights?

Some gadgets still on the drawing board would be a genuine boon to all households.

My research bureau is working on a 'B-chip' for television, which would censor instantly any appearance of Jeremy Beadle. It would also detect party political broadcasts, and replace them with replays of England's third goal in the 1966 World Cup.

But the most useful device of all would be a protective helmet, to be donned at the first sight of any tempting household gadget.

The object of desire would be blanked out, and a soothing but insistent voice would repeat in your ear: "Don't buy it... don't buy it..."

***

IN another misappliance of science, an American university produced a plan to give personality tests to cats before they are matched with an owner.

Cornell University's animal behaviour clinic is monitoring

40 kittens adopted from a shelter. In a year's time it will test its predictions of success or failure for each adoption. The clinic hopes that the results will help to save millions of cats from divorce by their owners on grounds of incompetibility.

The Americans are wildly optimistic in hoping to predict the future personality of a kitten. All kittens are cute, and for good biological reasons, to ensure that they get love and protection when they are small and vulnerable. The cute imperative will make kittens play with balls of wool, tumble over in engaging slapstick routines, get milk on their whiskers and generally pose for chocolate-box covers, only later revealing their adult destiny as a surly, sociopathic Cat.

Babies are equally deceptive.

But the plan for a feline dating service makes an even more basic mistake.

It should not test the cats but the owners. Indeed, using the term 'owner' would be grounds for failure. The proper term is 'partner and provider' and these questions should be asked of anyone seeking such a relationship with a cat. (Approved responses in brackets).

First, the home. The traditional standard, "big enough to swing a cat", has been replaced by something more rigorous: "is your home big enough to let a cat really swing?" This should be tested with a Duke Ellington recording. Is the furniture arranged to allow the cat to circumnavigate each room without touching the floor?

Now, for diet. What is your reaction to a claim that eight out of ten owners prefer a certain cat food? (Yes, but do their cats like it too?) Which of these is a suitable meal for a cat: your chili con carne, your refried beans, your tiramisu? (All three). If after sampling the chili the cat later shows the action highlights on your carpet, what do you say? ("Poor darling, I'll call the vet right away".)

Are you tempted by any of these names for a cat? Alexander Pusshkin; Napoleon or Cat Nap for short; Astrophe as in Cat Astrophe; Galore as in Pussy, James Bond's enemy; Purrdita; Valerie-Ann; Hecate; Moggie Thatcher; Eric Cattona? (No). Cats deserve a name which reflects their own personality, not one which shows off the cleverness of their provider.

Are you prepared to welcome, in any hour, place, or company the gift of a dead bird? Again in any hour, place or company (including a dinner party with your boss) are you prepared to accept your cat's need to perform intimate personal grooming? (Yes and yes).

Now consider the home-companions of Garfield the cat. Do you feel any sympathy for Jon, the nerdy human, or Odie, the frequent-flyer dog? (No and no).

Finally, and most important, are you and all your household aware of the difference between a cat and a teddy bear? (A teddy bear is a conscript, a cat is a volunteer. A teddy bear is on permanent duty to accept hugs, perform acrobatics, listen to personal troubles, and defend children against things which go bump in the night. A cat does these things only by choice).

These tests would do far more than the American proposal to prevent hurt feelings and hurt felines. But there is a still more reliable method to see whether cat and companion might be suited to each other.

Like motor racers before a Grand Prix, the two parties should try a practice lap.

***

AN AMUSEMENT arcade owner in Cleveland offers an electronic game where players whack traffic wardens with mallets. A Cheltenham man was recently charged with a public order offence for hanging a traffic warden in effigy in his van.

Drivers all over Britain display 'humorous' window stickers which threaten to electrocute traffic wardens or run over their feet.

These people should be ashamed of themselves. Traffic wardens do a vital job in inner cities. They promote movement and prevent motoring anarchy. They protect space for buses, cyclists and pedestrians. They regularly rescue lost children, cats and tourists.

But they could do so much more to improve urban life with a few extra tools.

Every warden should have a spray gun to obliterate stupid car stickers. 'Honk If You Had It Last Night': Zap! and it's gone. Wardens could deal in the same way with all variations of Halfwits Do It Thus-And-So and with 'My Other Car Is A Porsche'. (They should, however, spare the witty and truthful post-recession statement 'My Other Car Is A Repossessed Porsche'.)

They should be allowed to re-write with an indelible marker the many car stickers which are well-intentioned but manage to sound insufferably smug. For example, 'Warning: I Brake For Horses'... Well, goody-goody for you, but Warning: *I* Break For Coffee. "Pull Back And Give My Child A Chance" is another sticker which should lose its self-righteous overtones. A more honest and informative message would be 'Child In Car, Driver In Temper'.

A warden's armoury should also include an Electro-Magnetic Pulse gun, which could instantly silence any blaring car radio or stereo. It could also suppress any telephone conversation by the driver of a moving car.

Such conversations are not only a motoring but also a social offence. They make a statement about the driver: "My time is so important that I cannot stop for even a minute to gabble a lying excuse for lateness to my spouse."

A more peaceable weapon would be a packet of seeds, which wardens could plant in the thick dirt of neglected vehicles. Turning these into mobile window boxes would be a fine ecological alternative to writing 'Kleen Me' or 'Also Available In White'.

Finally, wardens should be encouraged to use their powers against cars which give special annoyance to the inner city.

There are few sights more joyous than the clamping of a stretch limousine, or one of those all-terrain monsters with wheels the size of life-rafts and more gears than an Italian tank in World War Two.

As for bull bars, which many MPs and peers want to ban... Whatever their merits elsewhere, there is no excuse for them in urban areas. Unlike Pamplona, our cities are not renowned for running bulls. Cars using the North Circular Road are rarely, if ever, damaged, by herds of wildebeeste. Parliament should allow traffic wardens to remove bull bars with laser torches the minute they appear in the inner city.

Such new powers and weapons would brighten the lives of traffic wardens and urbanites. But nothing would give both groups more pleasure than setting the wardens loose on *diplomatic* cars.

***

IT MUST be the most startling discovery in moving science since the wheel. London Transport revealed to a commuter group that 'heavy passenger usage' is the biggest single cause of unreliable bus services.

It is heartbreaking for a bus company to disrupt its carefully planned timetables by taking on passengers. Their selfish demands can often reduce a bus to a complete standstill.

Some of these people actually carry shopping onto a bus, or even children. Many others demand information or change from the driver. Some passengers do not even know the correct fare for their destination.

The late Lord Curzon once entered a London bus and demanded to be taken to 36 Belgrave Square. On being informed that buses had pre-set routes and could not be guaranteed to deliver him to his doorstep, he dismounted and never took a bus again in his life.

If we all followed his lordship's noble example, buses would hurtle to their destinations with the speed of Damon Hill. Some already manage to achieve this despite the handicap of passengers, providing rides as thrilling and stomach-churning as those of any theme park. Bus companies might try to exploit these commercially.

"Get Your Kicks On Route 66! Scream As You Hit The Low Branch! Spin Though The Air As You Corner At Speed! Say Goodbye To Your Seat… When The Driver Changes His Mind About Running The Red Light!"

Customers are a terrible threat to the orderly routine of

any business. London Transport is not alone in this discovery. Britain's water companies are — quite unreasonably — expected to supply water at any time of day or night, as if their customers needed to wash their hands like Lady Macbeth. Our hospital budgets are constantly threatened by patients.

But having diagnosed the customer problem, what can a bus company do to eliminate it?

It could persuade passengers to stay at home. Over time, this objective could be achieved indirectly by telling passengers to avoid rush hour travel. Since the morning rush is expanding forwards each day, and the evening rush is expanding backwards, the two will eventually meet at noon. At that point, bus services could be withdrawn between the hours of 6 am and midnight.

Bus companies could also consider introducing formal tests for bus passengers. Many drivers already apply these on their own initiative, asking would-be entrants to complete a 75-metre dash followed by a long jump. This physical test could be combined, like the Krypton Factor, with one of mental agility — explaining to a Japanese family of four the optimum route to the Tower Of London (or equivalent local landmark) and helping them to obtain the correct change.

However, there may be a gentler method of dealing with the passenger menace. Bus companies could provide a 'customer relations manager' on all their services. He or she could collect fares, assist the infirm or bewildered, restrain or eject the drunk or unruly, and indicate an appropriate time for the bus to move off. Many have experimented with such employees; they seem to make a real contribution to speed and safety and to be popular with drivers and passengers alike.

In olden days I believe that they used to be known as "conductors".

**

A CHRISTIAN Road Safety Association has been formed to combat road rage. Motorists of all faiths will wish it God speed (subject to any limits for the time being in force in pursuance of the Road Traffic Acts). But one may quibble with its slogan and its main recommendation.

"Care and prayer on the road saves lives" is both clumsy and ungrammatical. A more memorable slogan might be: "Drive with care, drive with prayer: Better late than Late" or perhaps "There's no speed limit on the road to Hell".

The Association should admit honestly that although road prayers are always heard they are not always immediately answered.

Every summer, on single lane roads, many people offer the prayer: "Please let this lost Belgian caravan driver turn left at the next junction." And does he ever? (No). Does he stay in front of the supplicants in the middle of the road increasing his speed only when it might be possible to overtake him? (Yes). How should they view this person? (As a test of their faith).

The Association recommends calm and diplomacy for victims of road rage. "Whosoever shall smite thee on thy right tail-light, turn to him the other also."

This seems too passive a strategy. The Association's members might instead try to quell an enraged motorist with a Biblical text, such as 2 Kings 9: "thy driving is like the driving of Jehu the son of Nimshi; for he driveth furiously."

The Association could offer its members as companions to motorists who get angry.

Road rage is always likely to build up when drivers are alone, with no one to share their just complaints about the unbearable behaviour of other road users.

After the right training, a driver's companion would know how and when to be *the first* to say things like: "Did you see that! Thanks a lot for the signal! Pizza bikes — they should ban the lot! Get a life, you sad geek! No, please take your time, it's only the fast lane! Why not start War And Peace?" If the driver showed any signs of appreciating these sympathetic remarks (for example, by removing his teeth from the steering wheel) the companion would then say: "I do not know how you manage to stay so calm."

On stressful journeys, the companion could try to divert a

driver's anger into harmless channels. This can best be done by making sarcastic comments on other motorists' taste: their car's colour scheme, its silly sucker-footed Garfield The Cat in the back window, the bumper stickers showing the naff places they have chosen to visit. Make a driver feel cool and he is more likely to stay cool — even when Garfield's owner makes a half-witted right turn.

In all of these ways, the Association could fight the good fight against road rage. Theirs will be an uphill task in low gear but they should say not the struggle naught availeth. The rewards of victory are great. As Proverbs 16 so neatly put it: "he that is slow to anger is better than the mighty; and he that ruleth his spirit than he that taketh a city."

Here endeth the lesson

Nine To Five... We Can Work It Out

A SINGLE European Market is all very fine, the free movement of labour is all very fine, but you cannot let absolutely *anybody* into your country to teach classical dancing.

So say the French, and the European Commission is thoroughly cheesed off with them. Refusing to recognize working qualifications from other states in the European Union, the French maintain their own legal restrictions on entry into many occupations.

Besides classical dance teachers, the French also have special examinations for sports instructors. In Britain (as witness any Sunday morning in any park) anyone who can shout is allowed to teach sport. This may explain why the French are now better than us at football (and indeed kung-fu). France even has regulations for furniture removers, again unlike Britain where they tend to be retired discus throwers or basketball players.

The French are also in hot water because they refuse to recognize Belgian hairdressing qualifications. Here they may have a point. Think of this century's only famous Belgian: would you want your hair to look like Hercule Poirot's?

Other European countries are even more pernickety than the French. The Austrians regulate gardeners: you cannot mow lawns in Vienna unless you are accepted into the elite cows of Grassmeisters (with uniforms and special swards).

In Spain they regulate bingo callers. It takes many years of study at the Escuela de Casa-Casa (housey-housey) before a Spaniard is allowed to chant: "Ochenta y ocho! Dos mujeres gordas!"

The Danes have special tests for church wardens and organists, an idea well worth copying in Britain. Would-be wardens could answer questions on Trollope. Learner organists would be allowed to stumble through All Things Bright And Beautiful, those on full licences could play the Wedding March and those with an HGV permit (Harmony at Great Volume) would be allowed to drive the Mighty Wurlitzer at Blackpool.

The British have generally steered a sensible middle course between over-regulation and a free-for-all. Broadly we control entry into trades and professions where the general public clearly need protection for their health, safety, property or money. Understandably, we insist on professional qualifications for mine surveyors, patent attorneys and orthoptists, and we are about to introduce a legal definition for osteopaths in case anyone thought they were simply people who hate osteos.

However, British regulations have some quirks of their own. They make it harder to manipulate a back than manipulate a mind. Anyone can call himself an analyst or mental or spiritual therapist, or even a priest (so long as he does not identify with any established religion). However, a public hypnotist must be licensed under the Hypnotism Act 1952.

Britons need no licence to run video games, but they do to keep a bagatelle board. This is presumably to protect young people and children from sleazy bagatelle arcades, whose addicts (Baggies or Pinheads as they are known in street slang) are such a pitiful sight in our inner cities.

Oddest of all, in Britain you need a licence to lend other people money but none at all to lose it for them, like the late Robert Maxwell.

However, one occupation in Britain cries out for regulation. It is nothing short of a national scandal that Bernard Manning is allowed to practice as a 'comedian'.

***

I COULD think of many better things to do with £250 than Plymouth College of Further Education.

It gave fifty of its students £5 each to return to the campus during their vacation in order to 'look busy' for a visit by the junior health minister, Baroness Cumberlege.

Even the most dim-witted duchess would have seen through the College's pretence. How it hoped to fool a bright-eyed baroness-for-life is beyond belief. When such people visit colleges of further education during student holidays they do not expect to be greeted by students.

It is, however, a sign of the times that the students were expected to look busy. In my college days, thirty years ago, a student looking busy in daylight in a public place would have stood out as an obvious fake.

An actor, or undercover agent, impersonating a student would have been better advised to chant a protest or a mantra, to play poker or a stringed instrument, to throw a frisbee or a tantrum, to start a magazine or a love affair, to argue about infinity and beyond, to perform satire, or to fall asleep.

Looking busy in any other activity was decidedly unfashionable and could earn a student the terrible accusation of being a careerist. A bouyant graduate job market spared us the need to keep up appearances and let us choose our own priorities: why change your shirt when you can change the world?

I do not blame the Plymouth students for acting as extras on their own campus (although a fiver is well below the Equity rate). But it would be nice to think that one of them murmured "Love and peace, sister" as the baroness bounded by.

However ineptly, Plymouth College is following a historic tradition of using actors to deceive important visitors.

In Russia, Catherine the Great's lover Potemkin built fake villages peopled with fake peasants to show her his success as Governor of her newly-conquered Crimean provinces. The term "Potemkin village" passed into history and his methods were copied by the commissars of Communist dictatorships, with Disneyland collective farms and factories, and chorus-line workers.

America, by contrast, invented the 'shill' — an actor paid to impersonate an ecstatic customer. Shills were first used by casinos. When business was slack they would arrange for an actor to collect a big money win and spend, spend, spend to encourage other punters. I have offered to perform this service for the National Lottery.

Shills spread into restaurants, with actors paid to be happy eaters in window seats, and into the movie business. Actors who could not get work in a film might well find themselves employed in its audience. After intense rehearsal they would be infiltrated into a 'sneak preview' in order to laugh and cry in the right places and to make ecstatic comments within earshot of real spectators.

Without going to such extremes, the discreet employment of shills by British businesses might help to restore the elusive 'feel-good factor' to the economy. They would also free many key workers from tiresome ceremonial and presentational duties. Why interrupt a brilliant scientist in mid-equation just to shake hands with a VIP visitor? It would be far more sensible to build a fake laboratory for such visitors and hire suitable actors as its boffins. For every Barnes Wallis we should provide a Michael Redgrave.

Our system of government would also benefit from substitutes. Our politicians waste a terrible amount of time on empty ritual and theatre.

We would be far better entertained and far better governed if Prime Minister's Question Time were taken over completely by Mr Rory Bremner.

***

RAIL passengers hoping to travel from Liverpool Street to Southend recently suffered an unusual delay when fifteen hamsters escaped from their cage in the guards van and had to be recaptured.

The methods used for this mission have not been revealed. Were they lured by lettuce or tempted by treadmills? Or did British Rail send straight for a cat? They were right to take no chances with these rottweiler rodents. Suppose they had jumped off the train and rampaged through the Essex countryside, putting Basildon to flight?

The delay must have been frustrating, but at least the railway provided a novel excuse.

Passengers have been fobbed off for too long with shopworn and hackneyed explanations. Frozen points... Fallen leaves on line... the wrong shape of snowflake... These should have been retired in the Steam Age.

Worst of all is the announcement that a service has been cancelled 'owing to a shortage of trains'. This is not an excuse but a self-evident fact: one does not need to be a trainspotter to spot an *absent* train.

A good excuse is a piece of good manners. It shows that we care when we have disappointed someone. Never perfunctory or mechanical, it should imply that the excuser made every possible effort to satisfy the excusee and was frustrated only by the inscrutable workings of providence.

No teacher, for example, should tolerate the plea that 'the dog ate my homework'. Even if it is true, it is boring and stale with repetition. 'The snake ate my homework' is a major improvement, especially if the pupil adds a description of a struggle to retrieve the homework from the coils of a reticulated python.

Such a description would meet the prime test of a great excuse — to require more effort and imagination than meeting the original obligation.

Repair businesses should remember this principle if an item is not repaired by the appointed time. Whether it is a wind-up bunny or an aircraft carrier, its owner should never be told that 'we are still waiting for the parts'.

The repairer should instead say 'there has been a dock strike in Sweden', and then explain how Sweden is the world's only supplier of the essential 'double overhead manifold' which makes the bunny or carrier actually work. It would, however, be a serious error to plead a dock strike in Bolivia. The customer may doubt whether Bolivia is a major-league manifold-maker, and may even remember that it is a landlocked state.

My new company, Regrets Unlimited, offers the first custom-made excuse service for individuals and businesses. It will not only invent excuses but help the absent-minded to remember them under challenge, and provide family trees for imaginary ill relatives.

For train failures, my company could offer far better explanations than escaped hamsters.

"We regret to announce a delay in the 8.15 service to Southend. This is due to the discovery of a colony of endangered natterjack toads at the bend near Shoeburyness... the result of a points failure on the Trans-Siberian Railway... because a butterfly flapped its wings in the Amazon..."

When passengers are immobilized, it is only fair to allow their imaginations to travel.

***

THERE is no greater threat to the British economy than the newly-imposed behaviour code for civil servants at Her Majesty's Treasury.

It urges them to start the day with a smile, say Hello to messengers, and apologize for losing their tempers.

If the Chancellor's own minions do not feel good enough to offer greetings to their messengers, what hope is there of a feel-good factor for the rest of us?

And who are these temperamental bureaucrats? I can remember when Treasury officials displayed calm and phlegm. The pound might tremble, but never their upper lips. Now they have tantrums over complete trivia, like £2 billion extra on the Public Sector Borrowing Requirement.

If the Treasury wants fewer outbursts of temper, it should cancel the instruction to start the day with a smile.

When people arrive at their workplace late, stressed and uptight nothing is more likely to send them over the edge than the sight of an inanely grinning workmate.

I am also deeply disturbed by the code's instructions to say "Hello." A clipped 'Good morning' or 'Good afternoon' to the messenger would be far more in the style of the British civil service. 'Hello' is American, and raises the nightmarish prospect of a reply in kind.

"Hi! I'm John. I'll be your messenger for the rest of today, serving you with the very finest and freshest of our paper-work. Today's specials are an update on the money supply, new opening hours for the Treasury canteen and tomorrow s winning Lottery numbers — just kidding!"

Like all offices, the Treasury needs a code of behaviour but the one suggested is a recipe for phoney cheer and false contrition. Its employees would be far better served by the following rules.

First, no one should be allowed to inflict on a colleague the story of his or her Awful Journey To Work. A special zone should be set aside for those interested in such matters. The Treasury should also designate a Viewing Room for the display of pictures of weddings, christenings, holidays, new houses, and prize-winning pets, vegetables or children. Such conversations or displays elsewhere in the building should be a disciplinary offence. (Airlines, please copy. Millions of passengers would pay extra to fly in a Non-Talking seat).

No one should be allowed to interrupt a colleague's nap, nor to comment on it after it reaches its natural conclusion.

No meetings should be held before the completion of coffee time (say 11.30) or during lunch (say 12 to 3.30) or when employees might be preparing to go to the opera (4 onwards). There should be no meetings at all on Fridays or Mondays, or during Cheltenham Gold Cup week or on any day of Test cricket.

These measures would all be cheering, but the only thing certain to raise any employee's morale is the sight and sound of Someone Else getting a rocket.

On really bad days, the Treasury should hire out-of-work actors to stage such events, one to cringe miserably while the other delivers a Basil Fawltian tirade of abuse: "You cloth-eared nitwit! I said 2 per cent on corporation tax, not VAT on chocolate biscuits!" (sound of smacked face).

Such a Code would produce the happiest Treasury since Gladstone performed his stand-up comedy.

***

A NEW battle of the Atlantic is being fought — in bed.

A team of American scientists believes that Western societies need more sleep. Drs Bonnet and Arand of Dayton, Ohio, think this would make us more alert and less accident-prone. Wrong, replies a British team. Dr Harrison and Professor Home of Loughborough University say that we sleep too long. We should get up earlier and take catnaps during the day if we start to feel drowsy.

The battle shows a startling reversal of cultural history. It was, after all, the Americans who created The City That Never Sleeps and the British who invented closing time. Clearly both sides are trying to learn from their mistakes.

The scientific argument can never be settled. People have different individual needs (or appetites) for sleep. Mrs Thatcher took only four hours a night as Prime Minister. Her predecessor, Stanley Baldwin, dozed off in Cabinet meetings. Mrs Thatcher's reputation stands higher, but it was Baldwin who left office when he wanted to. If Mrs Thatcher had slept through the famous meeting when poll tax was sold to her Cabinet, she might have done the same.

However, there is abundant historic support for catnaps. Alexander the Great was an aficionado, as was Napoleon, who invented a system to allow his soldiers to take them on the march.

Our greatest war leaders followed their example. Churchill's naps were stately affairs, in bed and pyjamas. Lloyd George's were more impromptu and often accompanied by a secretary.

Despite these heroic precedents, today's nappers face all manner of obstacles. The advent of the open-plan office — a living nightmare — has made them almost impossible at work. The risk of being videoed by a treacherous colleague and appearing on You've Been Framed with You Know Who is enough to keep anyone awake.

Worse still is the arrival of 24-hour financial markets. They ensure that vital decisions on currencies and commodities are taken by hype-stimulated hollow-eyed traders in the small hours. The world economy would be healthier if these people — and their computers — were made to sleep.

Insomnia is definitely on the rise, and traditional remedies are failing under the pressure of modern influences.

It is now impossible to count sheep without seeing a European Community meat inspector — and an angry French farmer. Trying to remember the names of Snow White's Seven Dwarves (a hard enough task at any time) is made harder still when Happy, Bashful, Doc and Co are joined by intruders such as Pushy, and Sleazy and Shyster.

Today's insomniacs are lucky to have the services of night-time television.

Modern social pressures against sleep have been eagerly reinforced by petty bureaucrats, such as Liverpool Council. They have introduced a by-law to ban snoozes in the city's libraries.

This mean-minded proposal discriminates against the poor. Britain's upper-classes have always treated a library as a spare bedroom. When the Victorians built gentlemen's clubs, in imitation of country houses, they equipped the library with deep armchairs and bound copies of Punch as aids to repose.

All over Britain's cities, people are starting to open Internet centres. They would do far better to turn them into Internap centres. Instead of buying an hour of useless babble on a Web-site, customers could buy the same quantity of healthy sleep on a Bed-site.

Given today's restless and unsettled world, one hopes that the American sloths win their current scientific battle against the British larks.

As Churchill so nearly put it, "Snore-Snore is better than War-War."

***

ONCE AGAIN a scientific survey has proved something we all already knew: people will hold outrageous conversations in a lift without realizing that anyone else can hear them.

Researchers recently took 259 lift rides in hospitals in Pittsburgh, USA. They heard hospital staff insulting patients and visitors, a doctor proclaiming himself drunk and exhausted, a male nurse described as too high on drugs to read a chart, all as if no one was listening. Forget chasing ambulances, a smart malpractice lawyer in Pittsburgh could set up shop in the lift.

Years ago, I used to eavesdrop a lift in a British government office. People would habitually reveal astonishing personal secrets — like the filing clerk who was hopelessly in love with the Queen.

His outpourings created bigger queues than Phantom Of The Opera. Sightings of him waiting for the lift would empty offices. A quick-witted manager transferred him to the sixteenth floor to give him more time with his unsuspected audience.

A similar illusion of privacy affects car drivers. At any long red light dozens will do things they would normally do in their bathroom.

However, the lift is much more than a source of overheard drama. It is also a setting for romance or ambition.

In Hollywood's great days many an excellent picture got made because a nimble screenwriter ambushed a studio executive in an elevator and 'pitched' the idea between floors.

Now the executives have private elevators and do not get ambushed. Instead they sit in their offices alone and make clunkers like Judge Dredd.

But many relationships still begin in the office lift... the shy smile between strangers, the discovery of each other's floor and occupation, of shared loathing of an office colleague, and shared tastes in paperback books. (I recommend PG Wodehouse for romantic 'lift-off' — guaranteed to produce conversation and an invitation to coffee).

The office lift is also a vital forum for the display of power.

If you want to look important in your organization, never, ever, be seen to touch a floor button in a lift. Wait for someone else to offer it to you. This will spread two useful impressions, first, that your time is too important to waste for even a moment, second, that everyone else knows which floor you work on.

With this rule in mind, it is easy to understand why office

lifts are so frequently stalled. No one is willing to lose face by pressing the button.

For that reason alone, all organizations could benefit by dis-automating their lifts and placing them under the control of attendants.

This would restore to a drab journey the elegance and luxury of a bygone age. The best attendants are not only fine pilots but expert psychologists. They have a sure touch with the magic lever: their starts and stops are always smooth and their warning to mind the step at each floor is always redundant.

But they also know when to keep silent or when to relax passengers with a light remark about the weather. They can assist office politics and office romances by arranging brief encounters, but they can also protect their favoured passengers from meetings with the office drunk or the office groper.

The job of lift attendant will not suit everyone. The hours can be long and the view is usually monotonous. But the dialogue is fascinating.

***

SCIENCE can prove anything, and a leading American psychologist has pronounced that gossip is good for your health.

According to Professor Ralph Rosnow, of Temple University, Philadelphia, gossip shows you to be sociable, interesting and well-accepted by your peers. But if you are off the gossip grapevine, you will wither away as a loner and a misfit and you will be the only one who is not asked to sing at the office party.

If the professor is right, we need urgent remedial action. Special schools should be opened for people who need to learn how to gossip and make friends. (A new version of 'the chattering classes'?)

For beginners, the ideal rumour is one which involves embarrassment or misfortune to someone rich and famous, or to a senior colleague at work. This kind of story will secure admission into any gossip circle. But the scale of the misfortune needs to be precisely calibrated. "The Office Manager's house burnt down" is not gossip but tragedy: it wig excite shock and sympathy and silence conversation.

But "the Office Manager locked himself out of his house in the nude" is ideal gossip. It lends itself to exaggeration and embellishment. Someone can add the story of his spell in police custody, someone else can reveal the strange tattoo on his right buttock.

More advanced students can be taught how to develop the following rumours. There is a fantastically cheap alternative to the petrol engine, but it has been bought up by the oil companies.

Giant creatures are breeding in the sewer system (choose from crocodile, python, reservoir dog or Jurassic raptor).

They Put Something in the office tea.

However, the rumour that there is life on Mars has been withdrawn on grounds of reality.

Gossip needs time and space to flourish, which is why it is dismal to read the recent report that 80 per cent of British office workers are not taking a lunch break.

The report shows that desk-bound staff become sad, depressed and rude to colleagues and customers during the afternoon. It was commissioned by Boots — the well-known sandwich firm — and it is therefore not surprising that it fails to recognize the real cause of these symptoms.

These workaholics are clearly suffering from severe gossip deprivation. They are not going to be cured by a three-decker bacon, lettuce and tomato.

Instead, these victims should be taken away from their desks for emergency rumour resuscitation — lasting a minimum of three hours, in a fully-equipped licensed restaurant.

Indeed, we could all benefit from this treatment, and the government should declare a new holiday called National Gossip Day. The laws of libel, defamation and scandalum magnatum would be suspended for 24 hours and people could trade rumours without fear of penalty.

Throughout that day every business telephone would

deliver a recorded message to the outside world: "I am sorry that there is no one here to help you. Britain is out to lunch."

Strangers In The Night

NOCTURNAL thieves in the Home Counties have been stealing entire garden hedges from infuriated homeowners, one of them 40 feet long (the hedge, I mean, not the owner).

The news, though dismal, is by no means shocking. Where I live, in a district the European Parliament chooses to call London South Inner, plants are stolen almost as frequently as cars.

Few of us Innards have gardens large enough to require hedges. But here in the front line the average life expectancy of a window box or potted shrub is about six weeks.

I myself have lost five window boxes in as many months. One was stolen before I had even learnt the name of the flower (it was small and puce). The police do not even find it worth recording the thefts, let alone watching ports and airports and alerting Interplant (the world's bio-cops, soon to be a major TV series).

After futile experiments with chicken wire, superglue and trained snakes I have been forced to extreme measures to defend my current window boxes.

Each is now equipped with a Biohazard label, with the following warning: "These plants were first bred in a research establishment for tropical diseases. Do not handle unless you have had ALL the necessary injections."

The warning has worked. My window boxes have survived into their seventh week. But I find it irksome to have to put on a full surgical suit, gloves and mask every time I want to water them.

I cannot understand *why* so many plants get stolen down our way. There is no evidence of a black market in the things. No one has whispered to me "Psst! Want a petunia, fell off a windowsill?"

I had a theory that all the flowers were being taken by the Mafia, as part of a contract on the life of a man with hay fever. But in that case, why did they steal the *plastic* ones too?

In my particular case I strongly suspect the PLO — the Plant Liberation Organization. I have received anonymous warnings: "water that geranium by midnight on Tuesday or face our wrath. Signed Wet September."

I have long been a target for the PLO. You've heard of Green-fingers. Meet — Deadfingers. My fuschia has no future, my begonia is a begoner and my aster is now a dis-aster. If the PLO have taken them to a happier sill I hope they are thriving.

But the Home Counties hedge thefts show a new and darker side of crime.

In the old days botanical thieves would steal a cutting or a seedling and leave the rest to the victim.

That is not enough for their modern descendants. As with so many other criminals they apparently need the further satisfaction of vandalism.

A nation where it is not safe to plant a hedge has made a deep descent into ugliness and has reached the borders of anarchy.

***

A NEW specialist squad of police officers has been drafted to combat the shocking rise in botanical crime.

Conventional police methods have proved largely helpless against organized gangs of green-fingered thieves, including the feared Petunia Brothers and their rivals the Sweet Pea Warriors. Using the latest anti-sneeze technology, they have snatched plants, furniture, ornaments, garden machinery, even whole trees and hedges.

Normal height requirements have been relaxed for the new police squad. It consists of highly-trained garden gnomes.

The plastic plods are the brain-children of a Metropolitan Police sergeant, Robin Murdo-Smith. In uniform, they keep a 24-hour-a-day watch against the bio-burglars and are an easily portable attraction in any part of the garden. As

Shakespeare so nearly put it, 'a gnome by any other rose would smell as sweet'.

The force is multi-ethnic, with a black sergeant, but Sgt Murdo-Smith will have to go much further to make them look like the police we know from television.

He also needs a hero-gnome, with weary good looks, a lonely sentinel in a dirty world. Although badly hurt in the past, he could be saved by the right woman — maybe the female officer-gnome, tough, wise-cracking, a lonely sentinelle in a man's world.

Another gnome would be the racist-sexist who is nevertheless a great cop, another would have an obvious drinking problem, and there would have to be a Flash-Harry gnome under suspicion of taking bribes. The squad would of course need a 'guvnor-gnome', who is a slavedriver but still idolized.

Finally, there would have to be a chain-smoking gnome in civvies — suspended for excessive zeal and fretting endlessly about his appeal board.

They might catch few criminals but they would make great soap together.

A similar squad could benefit other parts of the national life.

John Major, who himself had a spell in the garden gnome business, could see the benefit of gnome MPs. Silent, loyal, guaranteed not to rush in front of a television camera, easily collected by the whips and wheeled en masse through the division lobby, they would make his job much easier than his present collection of backbenchers.

If Mr Major wanted a vote of confidence in his leadership, he could put one up as a 'stalking gnome'. Cabinet reshuffles would be far smoother with gnome ministers.

Tony Blair might also see the merits of gnome MPs and candidates in his party — no dangerous ideas or policies, and much easier to fill the women's quota. I see a strong market for gnomes in the health service. Hospitals which were slipping down the new performance league tables could buy gnome patients, rush them through the wards and operating theatres and slash their waiting times dramatically.

Schools too could improve their exam results by importing

specially-constructed gnome pupils with a big computer memory — easy to teach and no problems with discipline and truancy.

The clergy could fill empty pews with gnome parishoners — guaranteed to keep their eyes open during the longest sermon.

However, an experiment with gnomes as television chat show hosts has gone sadly awry. The gnomes were too intelligent.

***

FAR from deterring biological thieves, the special squad of police gnomes have not even succeeded in protecting their own companions.

That is the only possible conclusion from the news that insurance companies have started to offer cover against the theft of a garden gnome.

Nowhere in Britain can now be considered safe for a gnome. Patios in Peterborough, ponds in Poole, rockeries in Rochester... all have suffered the loss of a familiar companion.

Who is stealing Britain's garden gnomes and why? Are they being resprayed and sold at dodgy auctions or car boot sales? Are there pubs where you can buy a mint condition bearded wonder for cash, no questions asked? Are the poor little chaps being shipped into slavery overseas?

If they are being kidnapped, one would have read stories of ransom demands, accompanied by broken-off pieces of fishing rod: "leave £1000 in used notes under your sweet pea or Gordon gets it".

Could there be a Mr Big of garden gnomes, a single, criminal mastermind assembling a private army of red-hatted anglers by the shores of a secret underground lake? Perhaps he is looking for some lost childhood friend. Or maybe he was frightened by a gnome as a toddler and is working out some obsessive private revenge on the whole tribe.

Then again, perhaps the gnomes are not being stolen at all.

They could be staging marathon rave parties in illicit dells. They may have run away to a better life (or at least a better place to fish). Some are probably in Ireland, with the little people. Others are sharing the high life with their cousins, the gnomes of Zurich, who annoyed Harold Wilson so much in the 1960s. Still others may have fled bankruptcy, as former gnomes at Lloyds.

The very existence of a 'gnome contents' insurance policy shows that they have moved from being figures of fun to objects of value.

The first British collector, Sir Charles Isham, was ridiculed by Victorian society for his claim that gnomes had souls. In a tragedy reminiscent of King Lear, his collection was smashed by his daughters.

But three years ago the Berlin Wall of the horticultural world crumbled away when gnomes were admitted to the Chelsea Flower Show. John Major's brother, Mr Terry Major-Ball, has led a passionate counter-attack against snobs and gnomeopaths.

However, their new status — and a flood of claims — will lead the insurance companies to demand new security measures from policy-holders.

Serial numbers could be stamped under beards, but a serious owner would want to have his or her gnomes electronically tagged, to emit a high-pitched scream if they were moved more than twenty-five metres away from their favourite mushroom.

In place of the traditional angling and gardening models, an Arnold Schwarzengnomer figure could provide a deterrent and display a little more animation than his film original. However, a Pamela Andergnome would be a magnet for midnight fantasists in shrubberies.

Celebrity and character gnomes can now be made to order, as actors, sports people, kings and queens, whatever the customer wants. It cannot be long before they break out of their garden ghetto and make their mark in the wider world.

A boxer gnome would fall over less easily than most of Britain's recent heavyweights. A tennis gnome would give Britain a longer period of hope at Wimbledon.

Musical models could help us match Norway's record-breaking performance at the Eurovision Song Contest ('Great Britain: gnome points').

In America they even have gnomes in the form of the Presidential candidates. But plans for a television debate had to be cancelled when the gnomes proved more popular than the contenders.

***

A CHEMIST in Kenilworth, Warwickshire, was a recent target of a bizarre gang of shoplifters who steal only toothpaste. They got away with sixty tubes, costing £100. The following further developments in this case are surely inevitable... Police issue computer-fit pictures of a smile they wish to interview. It is described as white, and of medium width, last seen with a damaged incisor, a worn bicuspid, cavities in the carnassials, and a loose right molar. People seeing this smile are warned not to approach it.

A professor of cosmetic sociology blames the media for creating an unnatural craving for white teeth. The toothpaste thieves should be regarded as victims of society, pursuing an impossible ideal of bodily perfection.

Police release hundreds of suspect smiles without charge, amid protests from civil liberties groups. A senior officer, Chief Inspector Gapp of Scotland Yard, predicts an early arrest of the Flouride Gang, but when pressed for further details he replies "my lips are sealed."

The Home Secretary tells the police that he is totally behind them but refuses their requests for personal mouthwash. He announces plans for a mandatory life sentence for all forms of "aggravated oral burglary." The Shadow Home Secretary lashes the record rise in toothpaste theft. He promises that Labour will be tough on decay, tough on the causes of decay. The Home Secretary says that dental crime is too serious a subject for a sound bite.

The thefts continue, resulting in new losses at Lloyd's.

Police apply a more scientific approach, targeting groups of people who might have a recurrent need for toothpaste. Chief Inspector Gapp says "the thief is almost certainly a person of limited abilities who is totally dependent on his smile." This is followed by a dawn swoop on the bathroom of a television chat-show host. No arrest is made and the police are forced to pay an undisclosed six-figure sum in compensation for revealing that the celebrity's teeth are not his own.

Baffled and humiliated (again), Chief Inspector Gapp is (as usual) forced to call in his infuriating mentor Hercule Poirot. The Belgian maestro travels to Kenilworth with his dim-witted companion Captain St Leonards (a late replacement for Captain Hastings who departed to test for the role of Forrest Gump).

Poirot says 'nom d'un nom d'un nom' several times while more toothpaste is stolen. Pressed to explain what he is doing he tells the captain: "I employ the little grey cells. I ask myself first, why it is that the dog did not bark in the night." They are arrested for plagiarism and are locked away in little grey cells. Released (on payment to the Conan Doyle Society) Poirot accuses himself of having been blind. "Why have I assumed that the thieves wanted to use the toothpaste? Suppose instead they were people of the type who hate to brush their teeth, who stole it to prevent it being used? Voilà, chef inspecteur, there is, your toothpaste gang..." And the police arrest Just William and the Outlaws.

(*published for the first time*)

***

IT IS hard to know who was the meaner.

The thieving toerag who stole the bicycle of a Grimsby paperboy in the midst of his vital mission for the local community.

Or the megalithic insurance company who refused to meet his claim, on the half-witted grounds that he ought to have locked it before each delivery. The whole point of a paperboy or papergirl is to deliver papers *at speed*. In America they actually manage this without even dismounting from their bicycles, serving colossal Sunday editions, with a hundredweight of supermarket special offer coupons, onto the front porches of their grateful customers. More than anything, this explains why America produces tennis champions and we do not.

The British do not go in for front porches. They expect their paperperson to dismount and cram their newspaper column inch by column inch through their letterbox.

The Grimsby boy's insurers are probably unaware that the standard British letter box was designed as an act of revenge on the newspaper industry. Its inventor, Mr Plinker, was enraged at his local paper for printing the wrong vowel in his surname in a list of guests at the Mayor's ball. After several years of obsessed toil, he perfected a device dedicated to the destruction of newspapers.

More than a century later the standard British letterbox still follows Mr Plinker's basic principles. It is narrow and shallow, so that a newspaper has to be folded many times over to slide through it. Simply to stay in business, many paperpersons have been forced to attend evening classes in origami.

The letterbox is fiercely sprung, to trap unwary fingers. It is frequently combined with a doorknocker, whose accidental activation will be answered by an angry member of the Addams family.

The Mail On Sunday is keenly aware of these problems, and immense care has been devoted to designing our newspaper as the perfect package. Many alleged competitors are too flimsy to force open the British letterbox. Other Sundays with their ludicrous pullulating supplements get jammed in the letterbox like Winnie The Pooh visiting Rabbit's house, and require an army of friends and relations to release them.

The Mail On Sunday alone has precisely the right mass and dimensions to cope with the British letterbox. In fact, each edition is tested on a special laboratory letterbox before being released.

Even after our painstaking care, it can still take a skilled operative a full twenty seconds to deliver The Mail On Sunday, and the insertion time for other organs is far greater.

If the Grimsby boy had obeyed the insurance company's absurd demand to lock his bicycle, the folks at the end of his round might not have received their Mail On Sunday until well after noon. Cut off from our superb news and sports coverage, our trenchant columnists and feature writers, our unique financial wizards and astrologer, they would have had nothing to talk about. Many would have been too embarrassed to go out to their pub or church.

I wonder too if the company has tried to negotiate a fiddly bicycle lock with numbed wet fingers in the teeth of a North Sea gale while under threat from savage dogs, cats and garden gnomes.

Instead of penalizing the paperboy, the insurance company should recognize the special problems of delivering papers on the mean streets of Grimsby.

It should replace his stolen machine with a tandem. This would allow him to take a minder on his paper round. And in his off-duty moments I am sure he knows someone who would look sweet upon the seat of a bicycle made for two.

***

A KIND-HEARTED thief of Sheffield has suggested a revolutionary way of protecting personal property.

He (or she) returned a stolen mobile telephone after hearing that its user could be sacked for losing it.

It is a mystery how the thief made this discovery. Perhaps the victim telephoned his (or her) mobile number and explained his or her predicament on receiving a reply. Far from being threatened with dismissal, such a quick-witted and persuasive employee should be promoted: he or she has a glittering future in sales or public relations.

Appealing to a thief's better feelings is a totally new concept in security. Several applications spring immediately to mind.

Jewellery cases could be labelled: Sentimental Value Only (and to reinforce the message: Try The Pawnbroker).

Instead of being stamped with a boring old number, car

windows could tell a heart-warming story about the car owner, making clear that the car is used only for emergency visits to desperately ill relations or to take deprived city children for once-in-a-lifetime visits to the countryside. Apart from deterring thieves, such messages have even brought tears to the eyes of novice traffic wardens.

Rather than screaming and whining uselessly into the night, burglar alarms could be adapted to deliver a pre-recorded personal message from an owner about how much each item of property means to him.

For example, a burglar attempting to remove the television set might trigger off the agonized plea: "No, please not the television! I don't have a life. You're taking away my best, my only friend!"

Under this system, a burglar could not take anything away without getting a room-by-room, piece-by-piece description of the victim's house. "Oh, I see you like the giant donkey. We got it three years ago in Majorca..." This kind of treatment could easily bore a burglar into escape or surrender, and those seeking maximum security could install an automatic display of the holiday slides of Majorca.

A sentimental security system might even end the plague of stolen garden gnomes which I described earlier and which continues to baffle the police of twenty counties. "Oh, now if you're going to take Gordon the Fisherman you really must take Isaac and his Wheelbarrow; they're inseparable..."

The ultimate test of such a system would be the return of the Style Enforcer, a bizarre burglar who roamed Los Angeles ten years ago. He removed objects not for profit but because he considered them tasteless or out of harmony with their surrounds. He was never caught, nor was any of his garish swag discovered. Even today it may sit in some giant underground thieves' kitschen.

The new security system would not prevent the Enforcer from carrying out his mission, but it might induce him to replace a stolen object with something in better taste.

If sentimental burglar alarms proved as effective as they promise, home insurance companies will insist on their installation. They will probably hire writers and actors to coach home owners in preparing their personal messages. They would also insist on an annual test of the installed system, which would be approved only if the tester left the home shaken by sobs.

The technology is there and the principle behind it is sound: criminals are more effectively deterred and reformed if they are made to understand the feelings of their victims.

And if anyone tries to steal *my* telephone he will hear my pre-recorded announcement: "if you have tears to shed, prepare to shed them now".

We're All Going On A Summer Holiday

CONGRATULATIONS to East Peckham! After deciding that it has no sights worth seeing this Kentish village removed itself from the latest South East England Tourist Guide.

Such honesty sets an example for the world.

Sightseeing is a gigantic confidence trick, invented by unscrupulous tour operators (such as Mr Thomas Cook) and greedy guidebook publishers (such as Herr Baedeker). They exploited the guilt feelings of Victorian tourists, forcing them to pretend that they were interested in culture rather than acknowledging their real reasons for going abroad: more sunshine, cheaper drink and easier sex.

The same guilt today drives millions of tourists to exhaustion from gawping at things which they would not cross the street to see at home.

While some sights are merely boring, others verge on cruelty. Take, for example, the Amphitheatre. Anything described as such in a guidebook will consist of a few sawn-off pillars, surrounded by some worn-out stone terraces. These terraces will be decorated by cigarette packets, sweet wrappers, crushed drink tins and decaying foodstuffs — a nostalgic reminder of Old Trafford at 5 pm on a Saturday.

A visit to an Amphitheatre carries a high risk of seeing a play in ancient Greek: three hours on the world's hardest seats, watching something incomprehensible through a haze of insects. I once saw 'The Flies' in these conditions and there were ten thousand performing the title role.

An equal hazard to the Amphitheatre is the Prehistoric Burial Chamber. This has similar décor, but in place of the Greek play it will produce a Danish student on a dig, to regale the unwary visitor with details of the boring and miserable life led by the Prehistorics.

Throughout the world, Folklore lies in wait to ambush the unwary visitor. In our country, it would be a kindness for the Ministry of Transport to put up hazard warning signs for Morris Dancers.

In Mediterranean countries, Folklore takes the form of dismal duos performing a song with more flats in it than an estate agent, about a shipwreck. Visitors may also be inveigled to join Exorba's Dance — a freeform, legwaving melée invented to create a thirst for expensive lager.

A close ally of Folklore is the Craft Centre, selling Paddington Bear costume jewellery made by left-over American hippies, itchy handwoven clothing, leather wallets into which no known currency will fit, and garish pottery artfully placed at a height where children are likely to break it. (After paying for such breakages, parents may enjoy seeing the fragments on display as antiquities in the local museum.)

The Craft Centre will often feature people in costume, reviving traditional crafts. Visitors may be induced to try their hand: if so, they will soon discover why these crafts died out.

More dangers lurk for visitors if they are lured into the colourful Old Market, the colourful Old Town, or worst of all, a conversation with the colourful Oldest Local Inhabitant (which will cost at least six drinks).

For lack of any other attractions, a visitor will be induced to stop and admire the View. This is the cruellest confidence trick: it invariably requires a tedious and uncomfortable journey, just to see somewhere else where the viewer would rather be.

All praise then to East Peckham! But its proud boast of being a sightless zone may rebound on it. A place where no one is expected to stop or shop, where no one is expected to fake interest in any attractions, could easily become a magnet for visitors.

***

IT WAS bound to happen.

Fuelled by high-octane rectitude, the American Congress

tried to ban smoking on any commercial aeroplane which enters or leaves the United States.

The proposal, promoted by an obscure (non-smoking) Minnesota Democrat, James Oberstar, and approved by the House Aviation Sub-committee, would bring about a startling change in international law. If it is passed, the United States would have awarded itself the right to penalize an activity by non-Americans flying over non-American airspace in a non-American aircraft.

The Congress might as well try to ban smoking in a British pub or a French cafe. The principle is the same.

I am not surprised at the extra-territorial arrogance of the US Congress, but I am depressed at their failure to grapple with the real issues of safety and convenience on transatlantic flights.

If they really cared two cents about passengers' lives, they would make the airlines fly them backwards — like a soldier or a VIP. They also might insist on a proper seatbelt, not something likely to deliver a massive abdominal punch in a collision.

The Congress might also look at that pre-flight drill with the lifejackets. If a modern airliner falls into the sea, will passengers really have enough time to strap these on, tie the approved double knot and stroll calmly towards the emergency exit, remembering not to inflate unless they are children? Or is this a fantasy, to soothe the nervous?

Apart from safety, Congress could do far more to relieve passengers' discomfort than playing gesture politics against smokers. Indeed, if they made flying less stressful, fewer passengers would need to light up.

Economy class over the Atlantic, trussed for hours into a tiny stall shared constantly with neighbours' knees and elbows, is living proof that pigs can fly. A serious Congress would lay down minimum requirements for passenger legroom. It would not allow airlines to steal more and more inches from passengers in order to jam in more fare-paying seats.

The Congress could also insist on a minimum width of corridor, to allow passengers a reasonable chance of stretching and walking, and ensure that passage to an urgently needed lavatory is not totally blocked by the duty-free trolley.

Talking of lavatories, the airlines should be made to provide a minimum number, at least three times that currently offered to economy class. If that eats into airlines' profit — too bad. It is sheer cruelty for airlines to ply passengers with drink and give them nowhere to deal with the consequences.

The Congress should also set down maximum temperatures for aircraft — to stop airlines heating them up in an attempt to sedate the passengers.

A caring Congress might also think about the needs of child passengers. The airlines now try to keep them quiet with goody bags and video games. If they really wanted to keep them quiet they might provide seats which would allow a child to stretch out and sleep.

Finally, a really serious Congress could have addressed itself to airline advertising. It would ban outright the false suggestions that 'wide-bodied' in an aircraft means more comfort (it means more people), that airline food is a gourmet marvel (marvel yes, gourmet no), that duty-free goods give more pleasure (and better value) than something purchased in a local market, and that flying across an ocean is a luxurious or even pleasurable experience rather than a necessary evil.

***

IN THE HOPE of making visitors feel more welcome, the West Country Tourist Board set up a 'charm school' for local hotel owners and their staffs.

It teaches them not to give visitors regional labels, like Cockneys or Brummies or Mancs, nor to call them grockles or emmetts, the traditional disparaging nicknames for anyone born east of Devon.

Two thousand people have already obtained certificates from the school, but as with A-Levels one can only hope that the standard has not been made too easy.

In the words of the West Country's most famous hotelier,

Mr B Fawlty: "life here would be all right if it were not for the *guests!*"

Too true. It takes far more than charm and a grocklefree vocabulary to cope with guests and their grotesque demands for food, drink, comfort and service. Hotel staff need a 'survival course', and I would be happy to design one for the Tourist Board.

Many years ago I was asked to test a special offer by a hotel to reduce its bill by £10 for each occasion on which its staff failed to deliver service with a smile. Arriving incognito, I acted for several days the most inconvenient and obnoxious guest since Henry VIII.

I let the bath overflow. I tap-danced on their best carpet in muddy boots. I rang room service six times in the night — the last time to change the picture on the wall. I complained about imaginary lost luggage and an equally imaginary mouse.

I forced the barman to look for a slimline soda water and upset several dishes of peanuts. In the restaurant I demanded to know the sodium content of every dish on the menu. When the wine waiter offered to draw the cork of my bottle, I snarled at him "this is no time for a sketch!"

Throughout this performance the staff concerned kept a smile on their faces, although the wine waiter's lip was seen to quiver.

From this primitive beginning, I have built an agency of Guests-From-Hell who can test the welcome powers of any hotel staff in the world.

I can supply any combination of fussers, complainers and worriers, including hygiene fanatics who will insist on things being scrubbed or boiled. My trained blaggers will remove cutlery, crockery, towels and bibelots.

My special Stag (or Hen) Night guests are guaranteed to shout, bawl, sing out of tune all night and fall off chairs. My Football Club Supporters will do the same but with additional fighting and damage.

My agency offers a selection of brattish children, many of them American, to make loud offensive remarks about hotel staff, food and facilities and to demand ice cream or video games at all hours. For extra payment, they will wreck the pool table. I can also provide any number of biting or incontinent pets with doting owners.

My Very Important Business Guests will insult the switchboard operator and demand use of the fax machine all night. They will also lose some Very Important Papers, which will require a search of every crevice of the hotel and of its garbage.

My foreign section specializes in running up large bills and then seeking to pay in Albanian leks, Malawian kwachas or cheques drawn on the Singapore office of Barings Bank. For hotels with sun beds I can supply an assault team from the German Bundeswehr. My Japanese are guaranteed never to say sorry.

If any hotel staff can survive these guests with their charm intact and no abuse in their vocabulary they will have earned not just a certificate but a jolly good holiday.

**

TRAFALGAR may have been a great victory for Nelson, but former Employment Secretary David Hunt tasted defeat there, when Britain's business leaders forced him to drop plans to celebrate it with a Bank Holiday. They told him industry was used to holidays in May and that was that.

If the government ministers took their rhetoric seriously about reviving the British economy... seizing the new markets created by the GATT world trade deal... fighting off the challenge of the Pacific rim... they would have abolished the May and August Bank Holidays altogether.

These holidays have little or no religious or cultural significance. One or more of them always has miserable weather, cooping families together in bickering and boredom and creating an artificial boom in the rental of rotten video films. The government should get rid of these Victorian survivals. They should at the same time legislate to give all employees three extra days' holiday entitlement on full pay — to be taken, by agreement with their employer, when they choose at any time during the year.

This proposal should allow British firms three extra working days a year. If these days were used productively they would add, by my estimate, about 1.2 per cent, or some £8 billion to our national output, without requiring anyone to work any harder.

It would save congestion and accidents on our roads and misery at our airports, and reduce drunkenness and crime at our resorts. It would give all the British people more control over their personal lives.

This proposal would leave us with only five public holidays (two more in Northern Ireland) — the lowest total in Europe. This would probably be unacceptable to our European partners and the EC Commission might order us to put some back. If so, the government should find some more original holidays to celebrate.

Victor Meldrew Day would be a special kind of Bank Holiday. The banks would cease trading but stay open solely to listen to complaints from their customers. If this proved popular the principle could be extended, perhaps as part of the Citizen's Charter, to government departments, local authorities and all other large and bureaucratic bodies.

I am sure National Free Speech Day would be popular. On this holiday the laws of libel, defamation and scandalum magnatum would be suspended, to allow people to say anything at all about any public figure. The cathartic value of such a day cannot be over-estimated — and we might discover whether we actually need our present libel laws.

However, the most daring possibility is to change a Bank Holiday into a Blank Holiday — the blank in question being Britain's television screens.

On Blank Holiday Monday the government would release an electro-magnetic pulse which would jam all television broadcasts, terrestrial or extra-terrestrial, and block the screening of any video. Twenty four hours with no television of any kind — twenty four hours for people or talk to each other, or make love, or visit someone or something they do not normally see — how's that for a national holiday?

***

THE GO-AHEAD Chief Constable of West Yorkshire, Mr Keith Hellawell, was unfairly attacked over his enterprising plan to raise funds for his force.

He hopes to open a police theme park. Through virtual reality visitors would take part in car chases and fly a police helicopter, and in real reality they could test a police skid-pan.

They would also see police marksmen stage simulated shoot-outs: this proposal caused protests after recent real police shoot-outs which left two people dead and two more wounded.

Two Labour MPs condemned the plan and skeptical officers have nicknamed it 'Plodland'.

Such negative thinking is deplorable. A police theme park could offer a first-rate entertainment package and become a money-spinner to rival Euro-Disney.

The tone of a theme park is set by its reception. Visitors at this one should be greeted by uniformed constables with the traditional police welcome 'Hello, hello, hello'.

Now for the attractions. The marksmen's shoot-out might be dropped on grounds of taste, but many other aspects of police work could be adapted into fun for the public.

Surveillance by Closed Circuit Television could provide a variation of the 'What Happened Next?' feature of BBC's A Question Of Sport. The action on a CCTV screen would be frozen and viewers would have to guess what crime was committed next and by which person.

Identity parades could provide another entertaining game: Where's Chummy? (Hint: try the one in the mask with the striped sweater and the bag marked 'Swag').

I like the sound of Interview Room — a race against time in which visitors would have three minutes to get a confession out of a suspect.

A money-back offer is always good for business. Visitors to a police theme park could be given a full refund if they spot their tail.

Theme parks always benefit from animal life. Children

would love to meet police dogs. But an invitation to see the Police Pandas would be misleading and lead to tears.

Cultured visitors would flock to a police art gallery, with works by Constable and Sargent. The theme park should also have a police restaurant serving truncheons and dinners.

One major attraction would be simple and cheap. Hit The Siren. Visitors would pay to let off a police siren loudly and suddenly (double rate for doing it at night). The police clearly enjoy this activity and it is time they let the public into the fun.

The Chief Constable was accused of putting forward a false, dramatic image of the police, and his plans are clearly influenced by television.

He would do better to revive a vanished epoch of television police. His theme park should include a section called Dock Green, after the long-running series which defined the image of policing in the 1950s.

Set vaguely in London's East End, each episode began with avuncular Constable George Dixon's greeting "Evening all." Its crimes were rarely if ever serious (although Dixon himself survived being murdered in the film 'The Blue Lamp') and they were *always* solved.

It regularly showed a teenage tearaway turned into a good citizen, without the need for social workers or boot camps, after a thoughtful chat with Dixon, who had recognized that there was 'lots of good in the lad.'

Dixon's was a kinder, gentler era, when the police were always friendly, never corrupt, and enjoyed respect throughout the community even from villains. Many people would pay to see it again.

***

IN A happy combination of commercial and spiritual motives, Thomson Holidays are to despatch forty vicars to Mediterranean resorts to minister to their clients.

A holiday originally meant a holy day, and the first 'package tourists' were the pilgrims who took their spring breaks at popular centres like Compostela or Canterbury. It will be a fine challenge for Thomson to restore this tradition and turn Benidorm into a shrine.

The vicars should not find it too difficult to adjust to their new mission. Many recent hymns performed in the Church of England would be far more suitable for Karaoke Night in a beach resort.

However, Thomson have made a serious error by confining the vicars to the Mediterranean. Their work should begin at the departure airport, when holidaymakers are most in need of spiritual comfort, and indeed divine intervention.

The Roman Catholic church recognizes the horrors of air journeys by naming no less than four patron saints for travellers: St Christopher, St Raphael, St Nicholas of Myra (alias Santa Claus) and most important of all, St Anthony of Padua, the patron of lost luggage.

Aviators have three: Our Lady of Loreto, St Thérèse of Lisieux, and most appropriately St Joseph of Cupertino. This humble seventeenth-century friar was famous for his feats of levitation and is an excellent choice to call on when one's plane is motionless on Runway Three.

Flying clergy could deliver a new grace for airline food: "for what we are about to receive, which passes all understanding, may the Lord make us thoughtful if not thankful."

Airline passengers in cattle class would join fervently in a prayer for a vacant lavatory.

Once installed in the Mediterranean, the vicars could offer appropriate lessons from the Bible to illustrate typical experiences from a package holiday.

Some famous passages might be slightly adapted. No room at the inn might become no room at the artist's impression of the future inn. The vicars might also explain why although it took God only one day of the Creation to put waters above and below the firmament of the Earth, a Mediterranean plumber needs rather longer to put water into the taps of a holiday villa.

At poolside services, the vicars could invite tourists to make a general confession of typical holiday sins. "We have followed too much the devices and desires of our own hearts.

We have chatted up those whom we ought not to have chatted up. We have drunk that which we ought not to have drunk, and there is no health in us. We have seen no sights and sent no postcards. We have coveted our neighbour's beach chair and left our towel upon it." (A German translation is available.)

"We have worn clothes of many colours and artificial fibres which are too small for us. We have brought shame upon our children by performing the Twist, and we have lied to them about our prowess on the high diving board. When they have tried to show us creeping things that creepeth upon the earth we have sent them from us, even unto the video games lounge..."

Thomson's new employees could also supply an even more important service. When Mediterranean wine, moonlight and stars have their predictable romantic effect, the vicars could marry the victims.

Have Yourself A Merry Little Christmas

IT HAS been rightly said that Christmas is the season of hot wine and room temperature vol-au-vents.

All over Britain millions of people who cannot stand their neighbours for fifty one weeks of the year try to tempt those neighbours into their homes with massive servings of this topical fare.

Why do they do this? Is it a sudden attack of goodwill or remorse over last summer's unreturned lawnmower? Possibly. Is it to get rid of the terrible liqueurs they got given *last* Christmas? Probably.

But the one constant motive for any Christmas party is the hosts' wish to show their neighbours their Christmas cards.

Their display is of course intended to reveal the Important People They Know. This function is so important that many hosts save 'celebrity cards' for years and redisplay them. Only yesterday I saw a genuine Clark Gable.

Others even resort to forging them, like the chap who sent himself a card with a heartfelt personal greeting from 'Paul Gascoigne'. He really should not have used joined-up writing.

Whether old or current, phoney or genuine, the placement of the cards is of paramount importance. Like the old Soviet leaders on the Kremlin podium at the May Day parade, the Most Important Person's card goes at the centre of the mantlepiece.

Lesser people are pushed out towards the sides — the further from the centre the more insignificant the sender. Relatives and other nonentities may be relegated to strings across the room.

It is here that a host can make a terrible faux-pas. Many a

social lion has been brought low by putting the Wrong Person at the centre.

Elementary mistakes can be avoided by consulting the Tables of Precedence in reference books such as Whitaker's Almanac. Does Madam Speaker of the House of Commons go nearer the centre than the Lord Privy Seal? You bet she does. But such tables are of only limited use to a card-carrying social climber. They do not resolve such tricky matters as whether a card from Mr Elton John should take a better mantlespace than one from Mr Frank Bruno. There is a crying need for a comprehensive and definitive almanac of social prestige. But until one becomes available I hope that the following rules of mine will be of assistance to anxious hosts.

Cards from Royalty still outrank everyone else's apart from Pele and Sir Donald Bradman.

Nobel Prizewinners outrank Oscar nominees and holders of gold discs but not Mr Frank Sinatra.

A card from Sue Lawley has no social value unless it bears a message *"Loved* your eight records..."

MPs nearly always send the official Commons card (one shows the House lit up in the evening like some of its members). This card should never be displayed singly, which suggests that the host knows only one MP and may even have joined his or her party to get on the Christmas card list.

Display of a card from Mr Oliver Reed may encourage guests to make improper public use of wineglasses.

If all this is too much trouble to remember, you could always arrange your Christmas cards on grounds of artistic merit. But this would take away part of the fun of Christmas and if your guests go away thinking you do not know Anyone it will serve you merrily well right.

***

COMPUTER games have become the blight of a modern family Christmas. An utterly unastonishing survey recently found that many children who play computer games show signs of addiction.

They display euphoria, withdrawal symptoms, and a tendency to abandon homework and social life.

Well, blow me down. But exactly the same disorders could have been found on the children's *parents*.

Euphoria? You bet — when a child's screen has a meltdown in the middle of Ninja Nerds II.

Withdrawal symptoms? I'll say — withdrawal to the 'unwanted guest' room just to get away from the sound effects.

Work and social life abandoned? Too right. No adult can work, or make sparkling conversation, against the competition of a computer game (have you tried phoning for a plumber while someone's playing Super Mario Brothers?)

There have been many recent studies of the victims of 'passive smoking'. By contrast, the victims of 'passive zapping' have largely been ignored. What happens to people who have to share their airspace, day in, day out, with a Streetfighter?

My preliminary survey has produced some dramatic results.

Nearly 100 per cent of parents have experienced feelings of extreme tension or rage in conjunction with their child's computer game. Such feelings frequently coincide with the intended commencement of a meal or a journey.

Over 90 per cent had experienced loss of appetite because a child's incompleted game had caused a meal to become burnt or cold.

However, nearly three quarters of parents had experienced weight gains through eating the child's meal as well as their own.

Two thirds claimed that a child's computer game had caused them to abandon plans for outdoor exercise. (This finding was disputed by children who claimed that the parents concerned never willingly left the living-room couch and could not, in any event, kick, catch or swim for toffee.)

Over half the parents surveyed had suffered some kind of injury in attempting to prise a child away from a joystick or console.

On the brighter side, 62 per cent of parents thought that their minds had been improved by their children's computer games — because they had to do far more of their children's homework.

But a whopping 95 per cent confessed to feelings of inadequacy because they had not been able to get beyond Level 3 of Klingfilm Attack. (The very latest in computer games. You are Airhead Slacker and you have to move around the house collecting snacks before Big Bad Momma wraps them all in Klingfilm...)

Every parent of a computer-game child in my survey suffered from a disorder known as Nostalgia Syndrome — an unfulfilled longing for a remembered era when families played Charades.

Many of these parents showed a compulsion to demonstrate their version of 'Bridge On The River Kwai' (it's a... whirl projector, first word... deal four hands of cards...) This group had experienced severe depression on discovering that their children had never *heard* of Bridge On The River Kwai.

Computer games are breeding a generation of lonely, flabby, anti-social misfits. And they are bad for children as well.

However, sentimentalists were mightily cheered by a report from Hamley's in the run-up to Christmas 1994. The great toy emporium said that children were turning away from the dastardly computer games and asking instead for magic sets, board games and, best of all, teddy bears.

Video games pride themselves on being 'inter-active'. Of course they are not: they make their users passive and obedient.

With their usual good sense, children returned to three toys that are genuinely interactive.

A magic set makes a child a performer before a live audience. It encourages not only manual dexterity but verbal and dramatic skills. When a trick goes wrong it can turn a child into an instant Tommy Cooper. All or any of these talents do far more for anyone than reaching Level 7.

A board game promotes company and conversation. Even the most primitive can teach mathematics and probabilities; the more skilful develop intellect and a sense of strategy. All board games teach fairness and sportsmanship (despite the frequent accompaniment of tantrums and tears).

But the teddy bear is the most interactive toy ever invented. He (or she) is an inexhaustible companion, a reliable comforter in fear and sickness, a confidant who never betrays a secret. A teddy bear is a partner for imaginary journeys, a sharer of jokes and fantasies, a foil for emotions — brave or timid, brilliant or stupid, talkative or silent as a child requires. A teddy bear turns any place into home.

If children recognize these qualities, and prize them more highly than the synthetic thrills of a video game, we have little to fear for the mental health of the next generation. And we can look forward to more sociable Christmases.

(*published for the first time*)

***

A UN PEACEKEEPING Force, not to mention a European mediator and a Contact Group of shuttle diplomats, were clearly required at the 32nd World Santa Claus Conference in Copenhagen.

The Conference, which meets annually to promote and protect the global image of Santa Claus (and friends), is normally euphoric. But the Copenhagen gathering was racked by factional fighting instigated by the Finns. Defying 132 other nations, they boycotted the Conference to support their claim that Santa Claus belongs to them.

They are determined to fight to a Finnish. The marathon dispute will continue until the very last Lapp, and the Baltic battlers have told the rest of the world to go to Helsinki.

City analysts are baffled why anyone should want to take over the ailing Santa Claus empire, whose financial controls would have made Mr Nick Leeson green with envy.

SC Enterprises plc, SA and U-L-Pay, was founded by the Dutch in the New World during the seventeenth century. They apparently merged the legend of St Nicholas of Myra with that of a Norse magician who rewarded good children and punished naughty ones.

Parents were quick to exploit this concept as a seasonal performance-related incentive scheme. SC expanded into world markets, also trading as Father Christmas and Père Noël. The characteristic red-and-white logo was adopted in imitation of the colours of Coca-Cola. (Really.)

The company is now a toy-manufacturing and mail-order business. Despite heavy losses, management refuses to rationalize its delivery system; it continues to guarantee delivery to all customers on the same day each year. Recent results in the wholly-owned Tooth Fairy subsidiary have been very disappointing. The company's biggest asset is its goodwill, but international pressures are likely to increase its financial problems.

The European Union insists on applying the Social Chapter to the hitherto unprotected elves in the toy-manufacturing division. They will get a minimum wage and maximum hours, with time off for picnics with the company's teddy bears. Meanwhile, animal rights protesters are trying to ban the use of live reindeer for the company's transport.

They have produced horrific accounts of over-age beasts being whipped to pull a heavy-goods sleigh far in excess of the permitted axle weight and forced into hazardous landings on unmarked rooftops. One reindeer, who suffers from an acute nasal condition, is even expected to provide lighting for the entire transport fleet.

In spite of these threats, the Finns still want Santa to themselves. The other nations have defied them by agreeing a universal address for children's letters: c/o The North Pole, Greenland. A truly modern Santa Claus should of course have an e-mail address. For something accurate and easy to remember, I would suggest: sc/kidweb/gimme/iwanna.

The Finnish problem might be solved by creating their own special character. Instead of Santa Claus, they could have Sauna Claus, romping through the snow in the buff and delivering presents to huddled families in huts heated by steaming Yule logs.

Even if this could secure peace, the Santa schism sends a depressing message to the world.

If a conference of people trained in jollity, philantrophy and mirth, whose universal language is Ho-Ho-Ho, ends in strife and sanctions, what Ho-Ho-Hope is there for the rest of us?

Yesterday

I WOULD vote for any Chancellor who promised to reverse one of the worst decisions ever made in Britain's economic history.

I refer of course to the decision to abolish the farthing in 1961.

For the benefit of sub-quadregenarians, the farthing was a small and beautiful British coin with the image of a wren. It was worth one quarter of an old penny, that is, *one tenth* of a present-day one, and it still bought things in my childhood — a small scoop of dolly mixture, sometimes even a licorice bootlace.

The farthing was a symbol of the enduring strength of a currency whose smallest unit had enough value to be divided into four. It was also a piece of living history — a coin mentioned by Chaucer.

Its disappearance, followed eight years later by that of its big brother the half-penny (pronounced *haypnee*), was a portent of the ultimate calamity — decimal currency.

This dreadful and unnecessary change gave Britain money with no history, no associations, no emotional value. After a generation of use it is still unfriendly and unloved. None of its coins have acquired a nickname. The lesser ones share their title with a visit to the lavatory.

It is no coincidence that the introduction of decimal currency was followed quickly by the worst inflation in modern British history. The new money was simply not worth saving. Moreover, it destroyed the familiar landscape of prices which acted as a psychological barrier against increases.

During this time (later to be known as the Bay City Roller era) I was working for the Price Commission, of happy memory.

We suffered deep anxiety over a threatened increase in the

price of bread, which would bring the standard white loaf to *three shillings*. Frantic schemes were devised to prevent the nightmare. They came to naught: the increase went through. We braced ourselves for riots in the streets. Nothing happened. The British people took the new price with torpor and apathy. They were brainwashed by the new currency. It was no longer a three-shilling loaf but a fifteen-pee loaf, a sum which looked and sounded trivial (like one-and-sixpence in real money).

Apart from its contribution to inflation, decimal currency has helped to destroy the mathematical skills of a generation.

Pre-decimal money divided beautifully into halves, thirds, quarters, and eighths. It was marvellous for sums. Children of tender years, without calculators, could work out how many sweets they could buy for six-and-eightpence if 4 ounces cost sevenpence-halfpenny. A few years later, they could go to a betting shop and estimate their winnings from a half-crown stake on a horse which came in at thirteen-to-eight.

Today's children have been turned into metricated muddlers, decimal zombies, prisoners of a debased currency in a devalued world.

If any political party got serious about the long-term conquest of inflation, it would commit itself to divide the pound into 240 and then divide it again by four.

A lost generation deserve money which gives them beauty and history and which makes them think before they spend it.

***

FOR CENTURIES, Britain's city parks were national treasures. They were beautiful, they were surprising, and they were fun. They offered city-dwellers the chance to enjoy space, water and fresh air, a great variety of trees, plants and wildlife, fine buildings, art and sculpture, sports, music, children's games, funfairs, sunbathing, and sleeping on the grass — all without leaving their city.

Not any more. Our city parks are being abandoned by the people they are meant to serve.

According to a joint report by the think-tank Demos and some consultants called Comedia (yes, seriously), city dwellers prefer to use their cars to visit parks in the countryside. They find them cleaner and safer.

The report, based on interviews with 1000 park users, found that city parents will not let their children go to parks alone, which both reflects and reinforces children's own fears of the outdoors. Another recent survey, by Handel Communications, found that children from seven to twelve now prefer to play in the safety of their bedrooms.

If parks lose families with young children they are losing their best customers. The Demos-Comedia (yes, really) survey found that city parks were viewed more and more as a haunt of drunks, homeless people and even teenagers.

Most people in the survey blamed the decline of city parks on the replacement of on-site park-keepers by mobile patrols. I fear that this may be a case of misplaced nostalgia.

In my childhood, the archetypal park-keeper was an authority figure to be defied and cheeked (from a safe distance). He is still depicted this way in old-fashioned comic strips, like the Bash Street Kids. He is a throwback to an era when children still wore jumpers and ties, and teachers still were identified by mortar boards and canes.

In those far-off days the park-keeper's main job was to stop people doing things. He enforced the notices which littered every park and which began invariably with the word 'No': No Ball Games, No Bicycles, No Skating, No Music, No Dancing, No Sunbathing, No Fun.

The park-keeper rarely deterred even young children from doing all or any of these things, and people a generation ago were far better behaved and more respectful of authority and convention than they are today.

Only recently I received a demonstration of modern manners when playing a cricket match in a crowded London park. It was interrupted continuously by straying spectators.

One young couple in particular took no notice of either cricketers or park attendants. They drifted, hand in hand, onto our pitch and lay together on the grass in a position I can describe only as extra cover. They enjoyed themselves there for about three overs. Being British, we continued the game and did our best to ignore them. When the ball was hit in their direction, fielders would jump over them or skirt them with a murmured apology.

Perhaps we were wimps — but if so, our cowardice reflected a general failure of modern society. People no longer intervene against outrageous behaviour in public places.

Maybe we should turn all our city parks into theme parks, recreating the world of the 1950s. People would stroll in Aertex shirts to the music of open-air dance bands. Children would wobble on Jaco-skates rather than whizzing on rollerblades. Teenage girls would give Hula-hoop displays. In exchange for forgoing modern pleasures, park users would pay 1950s prices in pre-decimal money — rediscovering the all-day fourpenny deck-chair and the sixpenny choc ice.

Without such a wholesale return to the past, our parks will be lost. It is useless to expect park-keepers to enforce traditional standards if park-users look the other way. If we the public are not prepared to protect our city parks, we might just as well turn them into car parks.

***

MAD Science has embarked on its ultimate folly. Computer whizz-kids at British Telecom are working on 'the immortality chip'. Incorporated into a wrist-watch mini-computer, the chip would be connected by probes to all the sensory nerves in the brain.

Every sight, sound, touch, taste and smell of the owner's life could be recorded, stored and played back.

They make it sound exactly like drowning.

Even if the technology works, who on earth would want it? Human memory is not a passive, mechanical faculty. We have been given a priceless power to edit our memories with emotion and imagination — a power which constantly enriches our lives and may even save us from despair.

As a cricketer in the sunset of a mediocre career, I use this power more and more frequently. It wipes out my dropped catches and turns my slow long-hops into leaping bouncers. It lets me play on Monday morning the innings I was unable to play on Sunday afternoon — gliding down the wicket, right to the pitch of the ball, effortlessly hitting the bowler over his head into the sightscreen...

The new chip would force me for ever to remember the stroke I really played, flat-footed, cross-batted, cross-eyed, and the consequent uprooted stumps.

The chip threatens us all with a lifetime's appearance on You've Been Framed! Every deck chair which collapsed under us, every garment which split around us, every dance partner we tripped up, will be recorded for a giggling posterity. The same for every fashion mistake we ever made, every car we could not start, every job interview where we made a complete babbling idiot of ourselves.

If a chip can record sensations, why should it not be able to record thoughts? That might wipe the smile off posterity's face.

The traditional scene in which the relatives gather in the solicitor's office for the reading of the will would be a lot livelier if they were first forced to replay the Dear Departed's memory chip. Uncle George hears himself described for the first time as a fat bore with a face like a dead gerbil. Aunt Mary learns that she was the worst cook in the Northern Hemisphere. (The solicitor would be well advised to edit the chip in advance, so that the relatives do not sue the estate for defamation.)

If the memory chip does come into being, I can see no reason why it should not be transferable from one person to another. Once recorded, someone's memories could be reproduced indefinitely and made available to others. This would open up some fascinating possibilities.

It would bring new meaning to the expression 'Get a life!' People could do exactly that. If they found their own life lacking, they could pop down to the local 'memory store' and browse through the departments for a ready-to-wear lifetime.

In the sports section, they could try being Pele, or Gary Sobers or Jack Nicklaus. Why would anyone buy a Steffi Graf tennis racket if she could buy Steffi Graf's actual memory of winning Wimbledon?

Cinemas and video stores would go out of business. Who needs to watch a Tom Cruise movie if he can *be* a Tom Cruise movie?

A transferable memory chip could even make Woody Allen's dream come true. When asked if he wanted to be reincarnated, he replied "Only as Warren Beatty's fingertips."

***

A GROUP of angry anglers have set off on a legal fishing expedition which could either net them a plaice in history or leave them completely gutted.

The Teeside Tidal Fishermen are taking the Teeside Development Corporation to court over an attempt to ban them from a 1000-yard stretch of river at Stockton. After the opening of the Tees Barrage, the Corporation sought to reserve that stretch for power boats. But the unhappy hookers claim that their right to fish there was written into Magna Carta — the foundation of English law — 780 years ago, and they are ready to fight all the way to the House of Lords.

I predict at least six weeks of legal argument, mostly in Latin and Norman French, invoking centuries of precedent in the fields of piscery, salmon-on-torts, and carpe diem. Both sides will have recourse to maps and Admiralty charts. An expert ichythologist will appear as *amicus curiae,* friend of the court, and in the interest of fairness an expert fish will appear as friend of the caught. These expenses, plus "refreshers" for counsel, could raise the cost of the case as high as a day's defence of OJ Simpson.

However, it will be money well spent if the anglers can establish that Magna Carta still has the force of law.

Such a conclusion would have surprised the original signatories, King John and his recalcitrant barons and churchmen. They thought they were settling a messy quarrel over taxes and property rights. They had no idea that they were writing constitutional law and entrenching civil liberties for future generations.

Success for the anglers would mean much more than destruction of the Tees Barrage. If Magna Carta is still in force, it will drive a coach and horses and the M25 motorway through many inflictions of modern officialdom.

Take chapter 13. "We will and grant that all cities, boroughs, towns and ports shall have all their liberties and free customs." This would render rate-capping unconstitutional, and all other restrictions by Whitehall on local government.

Chapter 30 reaches even deeper into everyday life. "No sheriff or other of our bailliffs or any other man shall take the horses or carts of any free man for carriage without the owner's consent." Try shouting "Chapter 30!" the next time you see your car being towed away.

Chapter 35 should see off the nonsense of metrication. "There shall be one measure of wine throughout our kingdom, and one of ale and one measure of corn, to wit, the London quarter, and one breadth of dyed cloth, russets and haberjets, to wit 2 ells within the selveges. As with measures so shall it be with weights." That settles it. The next joker who tries to sell me a metre of haberjets will get a fistful of fives (sorry, half-dozens).

All of these could and should alarm those in authority, but none so much as chapter 56. "If we have disseised or deprived the Welsh of lands, liberties or other things without legal judgment of their peers, in England or Wales, they shall immediately be restored to them."

If the fierce fishers of Teeside win their case, we shall be obliged to give the Welsh back their independence.

***

A COMPUTER recently simulated the voice of an eighteenth century castrated male singing star.

By blending and modifying a male contralto and a female coloratura soprano French engineers solved the biggest problem facing the makers of the film biography of Farinelli, Il Castrato, victim of a beautiful voice which was never allowed to undergo puberty.

The success will no doubt be a relief to present-day boy sopranos, but the rest of us should have mixed feelings about it.

The computer process which re-created Farinelli could easily be used to revive Elvis Presley. The King could live for ever, in the studio, without the need for sightings in supermarkets or alien space craft. Synthetic Elvis would never get bloated and sad, never become a crooner or 'family entertainer': he would be eternally raw and dangerous, a jailhouse rocker for each generation of teenagers.

But you never know where technology will take you, and if it lets Elvis sing for ever it could do the same for Des O'Connor.

If carried to its logical conclusion, computer synthesis would remove the need for any new entertainers. What chance would soppy Take That stand if they had to compete with 'new' releases from the Beatles?

Few would begrudge entertainers an eternal life. But the same privilege could also be given to politicians.

That was the spooky subtext of Forrest Gump. By expert electronic manipulation, the simpleton played by Tom Hanks blundered into history and interacted on screen with real Presidents of the United States. Some fretful critics suggested that this technique could be used to re-invent history. They missed the point.

Forrest Gump did not re-invent history. It abolished history. It abolished death. Forrest Gump proved that anyone, anything, which has ever been recorded electronically can be reassembled and reanimated — and made to look real. This technique (it deserves a name: why not 'gumping'?) opens up dramatic new possibilities for democracy.

It has become a cliché to say that politicians have become electronic figures. At the last election, nearly 100 per cent of the voters who saw the party leaders at all saw them on television. Barely 1 per cent saw them in the flesh at meetings and rallies.

Given that ratio, there is no reason at all why the next election should be fought between Mr Major and Mr Blair. In its main forum — television — gumping could easily recreate a contest between leaders of the past.

Nostalgic voters might enjoy a retro-election between Wilson and Heath, or Macmillan and Gaitskell, or even Churchill and Attlee.

With a little imagination gumping could even restore Gladstone and Disraeli. And if Her present Majesty would like a rest, gumping would allow the next Queen's speech to be delivered by Queen Victoria (or, with a little help from Glenda Jackson MP, by the first Queen Elizabeth).

In order to exploit all these possibilities I shall be launching a new political movement.

The Preservative Party will change the law to allow dead politicians to compete for office on equal terms with living ones. At the next election it will campaign exclusively by video, sparing voters the noise and nuisance caused by live rallies. If elected, its candidates will serve the nation without payment. Its campaign slogan: Why Get Stuck In The Future When You Can Vote For The Past?

I expect a landslide victory.

Space Oddities

THE LAST thing any of us needed to know is that Planet Earth is surrounded by a ring of cosmic junk, just like Saturn's.

Its finder, Professor William Reach, of the Goddard Space Flight Centre in Maryland, USA, believes that it has been around since the formation of our planet (4600 million years ago, last Tuesday). It sits about 300 miles above the Earth and has a thickness of 400 miles.

It is at first frightening to think that we could have missed a 400-mile ring for 4600 million years. But Professor Reach says that it consists of dust particles of one ten-thousandth of a millimetre or less.

That makes it miraculous that it was spotted at all, even with the help of NASA's Cosmic Background Explorer Satellite, against the competition from the celestial garbage which we ourselves have been putting into orbit since the first sputniks in 1957.

Whirling above our atmosphere, immune to decay and destruction, are flaking metal and paint and stray nuts and bolts from jerry-built space craft, leaking propellants, leftover astronaut dinners, and Heaven knows (literally) what else. With geocentric bad manners, we have also managed to litter the Moon and Mars.

Given our recent record, it is almost reassuring to learn that a tiny part of the mess around the Earth is natural rather than man-made. The professor believes that the new-found ring is the debris of a broken-up asteroid, and that all planets of a certain mass are likely to acquire one, like a spare tyre, in middle age.

But his discovery has dangerous implications — so dangerous that it might better have been suppressed.

As the witching year 2000 approaches, one crackpot group

after another is predicting the end of the world. Professor Reach bas given them all a new excuse. Even now some millenial Lance-Corporal Jones is shouting "We're surrounded by cosmic dust! Don't panic! Don't panic!", as a spaced-out Private Fraser murmurs "We're doomed."

Moreover, the new ring, like Saturn's, consists of millions and millions of individual moons. Do any of these have astrological significance? Could they explain why Aquarian horses never win the Grand National? Before announcing his discovery the professor should really have checked it over with Sally Brompton.

Above all, how can he be so confident that it is natural? No one saw it for billions of years. Maybe it was not there. Maybe it has only just arrived. Maybe it has been put around us *by aliens*. What are they up to? Will they try to make the ring denser, and if so, why? To blot out the Sun and put us in the deep freeze? Or are they just trying to build a parking lot? (If Professor Reach owns the movie rights to the ring, I will make him a fabulous offer.)

Even if it is natural, Professor Reach's discovery has wrecked the image of the Earth. We can no longer see it as the shining sapphire of the famous NASA photograph from the Moon.

Our planet is no longer a jewel. It is a neglected ornament in a spare room of the Universe, with a layer of old dust.

(Space garbage claimed its first victim in 1996 when an expensive French spy satellite, the Cerise, was destroyed by a fragment of orbiting debris)

***

THE EARTH has sent a New Year message to the rest of the Universe. Twenty-two years after its launch, the Pioneer XI spacecraft is crossing the known frontier of the Solar System.

It may discover Planet X, the deep-frozen giant lurking millions of miles beyond Pluto. The first thing it will find there will be a sunbed with a German towel on it. But we will never know, because NASA decided to switch off the spacecraft's power supply.

Pioneer XI is famous for bearing a gold plaque, saying "Hey, we're over here" to any aliens who find it. The plaque was designed by the astronomer Carl Sagan, and shows the equivalent of an Underground map of the Solar System with a picture of a naked man and woman.

In fact, as Professor Sagan himself recognized in an excellent novel, the Earth has been sending out signals since long before Pioneer XI — through television. Transmissions have leaked through the Earth's ionosphere and have radiated, unstoppably, through outer space at the speed of light. This means that when aliens do arrive here, the first thing they will ask is "Whatever happened to Kylie Minogue?"

However, it is a good moment to think what might happen if Pioneer XI fulfils its mission. What sort of aliens would we like it to find?

My first choice would be the InterGalactic Refuse Service. They could come and collect the appalling junk which we have already scattered around our planet.

This junk forced the space shuttle Columbia to shut its normally-open cargo doors, in case of damage to its equipment. It is a sorry thing when driving in space is more dangerous than driving in Miami, and if aliens could clear up this garbage I would be happy to leave them a tip next year in an orbiting Christmas box.

My next choice would be Mr Spock. The super-logical Vulcan who has guided so many Star Trek missions all over the wildest reaches of hype-space should able to quote me the cheapest fare on a British train journey.

ET might be able to teach me how to use my portable phone — or even how to work out its tariff.

Darth Vader would be a popular replacement for Jeremy Beadle.

Best of all would be a visit from the folks in '2001' with the portable black holes. They would make a killing in the travel business: imagine getting to the back of Betelgeuse and beyond without once having to eat airline food.

However, the chances are that Pioneer XI will not lead us to anyone interesting. Think again about that underground map. It shows the Earth to be a small suburban station on a branch line of the Universe. People do not make special journeys to that kind of station: they use them because they live or work nearby — or to visit people they know.

If aliens do want to come here they will be very like us. They will have better space transport than we do: in every other respect they may have all of our problems and limitations.

With Pioneer XI we have spent twenty two years sending an expensive postcard to relatives we probably will not like and who have nothing to talk about except their car.

***

IT WAS a scene of pure movie madness.

Picture the huge, gleaming Discovery space shuttle waiting for launch at Cape Canaveral. The high priests of Mission Control start the final countdown, with the familiar hypnotic mixture of numbers and astro-babble. "Enter launch mode... forty-five seconds... commence ignition sequence... thirty seconds... all systems activated... ten... nine... eight..."

Suddenly a horribly familiar sound interrupts their litany. "Peck... peck... peck...Ya-pa-pa-*dee*-da!"

"Mission abort! It's that damn woodpecker again!"

Mad but true... Woody Woodpecker and his chums have caused havoc with a vital space shuttle mission. They have managed to peck holes in Discovery's fuel tank — no less than seventy one, the largest of them four inches in diameter.

It is a powerful symbol for our age that the world's most advanced (and most costly) technological project should be frustrated by bird brains.

But, true to the immortal cliché, scientists are baffled. They simply cannot keep the woodpeckers at bay. Their predicament is no surprise to admirers of Woody Woodpecker, whose cartoon life shows his ability to survive blows from giant mallets, deadly poisons (labelled 'Deadly Poison'), point blank gunshots, and even explosions.

The woodpeckers' success should make us think twice about buying any of the products which are 'spin-offs' from the exploration of space.

These blessings include the non-stick frying pan, the digital watch, the miniature vacuum cleaner, the survival blanket, the ballpoint pen which writes upside down and even the ring-pull on drink cans. Every time we use one of them, every time we see any new gizmo advertised with the words 'incorporating the latest space-age technology', we should remember that it came from the same team who could not build a peckerproof fuel tank.

The woodpeckers should also remind us that Nature has a long track record of victory over the artifice of Man.

Dunsinane castle, which survived Macbeth and his lady, witchcraft and Macduff's army, is now being undermined by rabbits. Insects have successfully resisted successive generations of more powerful chemicals. The locust is even more devastating today than it was in Biblical times.

Even molluscs have been more than a match for Man. Take, for example, the common slugs who have been eating the petunias in my window box.

The common slug is not one of nature's Masterminds. On the scale of creature intelligence it ranks only one place above chat-show host. But somehow a group of common slugs has managed regularly to climb a sheer wall, negotiate a dangerous overhang and evade a minefield of slug pellets to stage a dinner party in my petunias. How do they do it — by parachuting?

However, in pride of place as Nature's standard-bearer is the world's remotest tree. It stands alone in the Sahara desert, at least a thousand miles from its nearest botanical companion. In the deadpan words of the Guinness Book Of Records, "it has survived several collisions from trans-continental lorries."

It is some kind of triumph for Man to propel a heavy vehicle into the only traffic obstruction in an area greater than π times 1000 times 1000, or roughly 3.142 million, square miles.

But Nature was still the ultimate victor. It remains only for

Man to signal surrender by building a service facility around the tree. "Last tree for 1000 miles. No dogs or football coaches."

As for NASA, they clearly need expert help if they are to outwit Woody Woodpecker. They should send at once for Bugs Bunny.

***

A GENERATION has grown up since Neil Armstrong fluffed the most important line in history.

"One small step for man: one giant leap for mankind": imagine coming all that way and forgetting the indefinite article. By leaving out the 'a' before 'man' be ensured that the first words spoken on another world should be gibberish. No one should be too hard on Mr Armstrong. He had spent months and months talking astro-babble and acronyms; it was clearly too much to expect him to switch suddenly into English.

If NASA had wanted deathless speech from the lunar surface they should have had him dubbed by Laurence Olivier.

Even if delivered correctly, it was not much of a line to begin with. The scriptwriters could have come up with something a lot snappier.

Imagine Mr Armstrong scooping some of the surface and exclaiming "Hey, this would be great with crackers and celery!" Or maybe: "Great food, shame about the atmosphere." Perhaps, on second thoughts, not: only a Marx brother could have got away with them.

But a simple "Hi there! What's your name?" would have had an electrifying effect on his Earthly audience.

But seriously… Mr Armstrong should have looted the poets and songwriters. Duke Ellington would have provided an appropriate boast "I'm riding on the moon and dancing on the stars." Even more accurately, "Blue Moon, now you're no longer alone" would have been a nice switch on Rodgers and Hart. Stepping onto the airless world, Mr Armstrong could also have adapted Simon and Garfunkel: "I have heard the sound of silence".

For simple good manners, Dorothy Parker's epigram-epitaph could not have been bettered: "Excuse my dust."

On a philosophic note he could have tried Thomas Hardy: "What do you think of it, Moon, as you go? Is life much or no?" Or more cheerfully, Falstaff's manifesto to Prince Hal: "let men say we be men of good government, being governed, as the sea is, by our noble and chaste mistress the moon."

Or most joyously of all, John Donne's version of Genesis: "As soon as God had made light he was glad of it, glad of the sea, glad of the earth, glad of the sun and moon and stars, and he said of every one, It is good."

Yet my favourite alternative line for Mr Armstrong comes from an unknown modern hand. It was submitted to NASA in Houston as part of a worldwide search for words to celebrate the moon landing, and was published in a list of 'rejects'.

It was more elegant than the one the astronaut was to garble, and expressed a truth both metaphorically and literally about that first step onto a world without wind or water to change its landscape.

"Man has left a footprint which can never be erased."

If I Ruled The World
(a political broadcast on behalf of the Bolshie Party)

IN A savage attack on Big Government, the United States Senate recently voted to abolish the Board of Tea Experts, a Federal agency which since 1897 has tasted and monitored imported tea.

On its record, the agency was certainly ripe for the chop. In nearly a hundred years it has been unable to persuade the Americans to drink tea. (Their iced version is an amusing little beverage, but it is not tea within the meaning of the Act).

If the Americans find that they still need people to test tea for them, they should look no further than the British civil service. Its members have both aptitude and experience and many would welcome the chance to sip for dollars.

It would of course be no easy task to establish a Civil Service tasting unit. The mandarins would have to set up a tasters' selection board, steered by a steering committee and overseen by an oversight committee, with an appeals board on standby for aggrieved non-selections. Needless to say, all of these people would themselves require tea.

To guarantee real expertise in brewing, a tea-tasting unit would have to include a former sergeant-major. It should also have a special test for biscuit dunkers: they will be expected to remember things past since their early childhood.

We should not mock the Americans for having a tea-tasting quango. We British had 1345 of them when the government last counted, and they include some wonders.

Take, for example, the Apple and Pear Research Council. Once famous for its Conferences, this body's will to exist is beginning to crumble. There is also a Seed Potato Development Council, but only for Scotland. How does England manage without one?

We also have a Marshall Aid Commemoration Commission, still working out bow to commemorate General Marshall's initiative forty eight years later. Good thing we did not have a Nelson Commemoration Commission: Trafalgar Square would look empty.

I do not know if the Great Britain China Centre deals with Beijing or Wedgwood, but either way I am sure it is necessary.

British quangoes used to be the preserve of the 'great and the good'. Not any more: the government has invited 'ordinary members of the public' to volunteer for service. The take-up so far has been disappointing, almost certainly because current quangoes are so deadly dull (except for devotees of the Scottish seed potato).

I therefore suggest the creation of three new British quangoes.

The British Beer Development Council is self-explanatory. It may have a few initial hiccups but it should soon settle and it will attract people of standing (their rounds).

The Holiday Standards Board would test the claims of holiday brochures and set up a grading system with minimum standards. This Board would clearly require special expertise in the Indian Ocean region, with (literally) in-depth water inspections around Sri Lanka, the Maldives, Mauritius and the Seychelles.

Finally, the National Lottery Counselling Service would assist winners to spend their money without guilt and stress. Its members would dispose of begging letters and newly-discovered relatives and childhood friends, and offer expert advice on house, car and racehorse purchase, travel, wardrobe and general lifestyle spending, accompanying winners whenever necessary.

I am certain that these quangoes would bring new talent into Britain's public life.

***

IT WAS really a bit cheeky of Germany to want to name the common European currency as well as manage it.

Any country which signs up for the new currency gives up its right to devalue against the Germans. That is wunderbar for German exports, German industry and German jobs. They should be grateful.

But no, the Germans want to have their cake and name it too. Still, the new currency does deserve a better name than the écu, which sounds like a failed attempt at an obscenity. (Écu! And ache you too, you prat!) It needs a name which conveys a sense of value. How about the yen?

But seriously... a country can make itself a laughing stock by choosing the wrong name for its currency.

The Vietnamese have created endless cheap jokes for English-speaking money markets with the dong. If the dong goes up or down or gets hit the dealers are in stitches.

The Laotians are scarcely better off with the kip. "Where are you going?" asks Mrs Lao of Mr Lao. His reply "To the bank to get some kip" is easily mistaken for sarcasm, leading to tears and flying plates.

But the daftest currency must be the Korean won. This is almost impossible to say in the singular. Try this sentence for yourself. "I bought a lottery scratchcard and won one won."

A few lucky countries have currency with charm like the Guatemalan quetzal, named after its exotic national bird. Gorgeous money the quetzal — and very useful for Scrabble.

From that point of view, it would be helpful to call the Euro-currency the quidzin, divided into a hundred jekus.

However, the new Central Bank will probably insist on something more dignified. We British could offer plenty of fine coins we are not using any more.

Republicans would reject the sovereign, atheists the angel and classless society proponents the noble. But no faction would object to the groat.

An Anglo-Dutch-Italian alliance could press for the florin. The Scots and the Greeks might unite around the wee drachma. The Spanish might secure Irish support for the doubloon. (However, the doubloon was divided into pistoles, which would cause deep offence to pacifists.) But I have a terrible feeling that in trying to offend nobody the authorities will end up calling the new currency Europa, which is weak, implausible and already in use for a goddess and a satellite of Jupiter.

However, there is one name for the new currency which would pay tribute to a founder of European unity and make an elegant play on words in several European languages.

They should call it the Monnet.

(The then French Finance minister, M Alain Madelin, responded with some enthusiasm to this suggestion. But the new currency acquired the utterly mediocre — and unfinished — name of the Euro).

***

ARGENTINA's tramps (pardon me, the correct term now is 'dis-careered ambulant persons') held a summit meeting at the fashionable Mar del Plata resort — to demand that May 2 should be declared a World Day of Idleness.

Three generations ago, May 1 was stolen by Stalin to stage pompous (and lying) tributes to his regimented, rightless workers. It would therefore be cheering to use the day after as a celebration of the world's slackers, a sloppy, sleepy, sham-bolic celebration in which no one would be allowed to get up and march.

A few minutes' thought (in a horizontal position) will provide many reasons for Slacker pride.

True Slackers are non-violent, and have never caused a world war or even an exchange of sharply-worded diplomatic notes. They commit few crimes other than the watching of television without a licence.

Although their local and personal environment may be squalid, the global environment benefits from their immobi-lity, which saves transport and energy resources. Slackers also help the planet by endlessly recycling second-hand clothes for their eclectic and nostalgic wardrobes. Slacker T-shirts are where old rock groups go to die: many a youthful beergut hides under a Thin Lizzy.

Slackers do valuable unpaid labour testing the strength

and resistance to food stains of beds, chairs and couches. They sustain the video rental and pizza industries.

Their shopping habits (rare and everything possible ordered by telephone) make them less likely to buy Lottery tickets, thus giving greater winning chances to hardworking joes like you and me.

They provide a television audience (and thereby life-giving income and sponsorship) for insanely dull sports such as darts and American pool. By watching daytime television they also keep chat-show hosts and soap opera actors in the only jobs they could possibly do.

Above all, dedicated Slackers vacate jobs for people who really want to do them. In a world where billions are genuinely seeking work we should be prepared to reward, not penalize, those who are genuinely seeking idleness.

Working Slackers are a social blight and an economic error. They depress output in any firm which harbours them, teaching their colleagues the pleasures of sloth, absenteeism and task-avoidance.

By virtue of Murphy's famous Law, a working Slacker is certain to come into contact with an important customer or to be left in sole charge of some vital operation. Slackers are far better occupied on the couch at home than as shop assistants, waiters or nuclear safety officers.

Slackers at work often turn into Skivers, inventing elaborate reasons for absence and conning doctors into issuing sick notes. Instead of using their imaginative powers on symptoms, emergencies and frail relatives, such Slackers should be home writing the great twenty-first century novel.

Slackers have at last received their reward, a toy beyond their wildest dreams. It lets them escape into an endlessly-expanding world of entertainment and fantasy, but requires no physical effort and can be changed the moment it becomes boring or mentally demanding. It lets them 'talk' to strangers without the effort of speech or the obligation to share food or drink or even real names and identities.

If May 2 does become World Slacker Day, they will hold the parades on the Internet.

***

THE GOVERNMENT recently published a most important 'league table' of exam results. It shows that Britain's candidates performed rather well in getting posts in the bureaucracy of the European Commission.

Needless to say the Germans were first in the race for these well-paid deckchairs, but our boys and girls were a highly creditable second, taking 15 per cent of the Euro-jobs on offer.

The government also gave details of the basic exam which they had to pass. It reads like a Mastermind final: eclectic general knowledge questions and a compulsory special subject of Europe.

But the government chose not to reveal the *advanced* exam, for candidates seeking the most senior positions in Brussels. This perhaps was wise, since the questions and marks were as follows:

1) What is the difference between an EMU and an ECU? (40 marks)

2) What is subsidiarity, and what should you do if it happens to your house? (60 marks)

3) Kanst du help me mit eine small loan, kamerad, ich bin expecting eine postal order on Thursday? (100 marks would do. Danke)

4) Examine the case for putting the European Central Bank in London and explain why it will be located in Frankfurt (40 billion marks cannot be wrong)

5a) You are chosen to be President of the European Commission. Explain your plans for ending national sovereignty and moving to a Federal Europe.

5b) You are chosen to be President of the French Republic. Explain your plans for resisting a Federal Europe and defending national sovereignty. *Candidates must answer both parts of the question.* (500 francs)

6) After five years in charge of world trade negotiations you are transferred to a new post in the office stationery division. Reconsider your position and give your reason for staying on (250,000 marks, tax free)

7) Study the following extract from the latest European Directive on paperclips and translate it from Danish into Portuguese (200 escudos or small brandy)

8) An audit reveals a European surplus equivalent to over two years' supply of sugar, flour, eggs, dairy produce and fortified wine. Choose between these ways of getting rid of them:
   a) pay the Russian mafia to take them away (100 marks)
   b) make a sherry trifle as big as Belgium (100 marks, give recipe)
   c) end European farm subsidies and introduce free trade in agricultural produce (zero marks, are you mad?)

9) You are put in charge of a task force to tackle bureaucracy and over-regulation in Europe. Make your staff application (1000 marks for each post required) and explain how many jobs will be given to nationals of each member-state ("L'Irlande, dix postes"... "Ireland, ten posts")

10) You decide to hold a 'working lunch' for the steering committee of this task force. Study the enclosed menu from La Grande Bouffe restaurant (trois étoiles Michelin) and select six courses. Explain your choice of wines. (10,000 marks American Express? Ça ira gentiment...)

Candidates will write on all sides of each question. The results of the examination will be postponed until the last possible summit, when any dispute over places is to be resolved in favour of the candidate from Luxembourg.

***

THE VOTERS of Swale, in Kent, delivered a short, sham, shock election message to all of Britain's politicians.

Only thirty five of them bothered to turn up for a by-election to fill a vacant seat on the local town council — and one even managed to spoil his or her ballot paper. The turnout, of 4 per cent, is believed to be the lowest recorded in British politics since the days of rotten boroughs.

The thumping 96 per cent vote for the Stay-At-Home party could be interpreted as a positive decision to try life without a councillor. If so, they can feel that they were robbed by the thirty five political obsessives who insisted on voting.

What if everyone had stayed at home? Britain's voting laws fail to cater for this possibility. Our politicians clearly could not bear to imagine an election in which nobody wanted to vote — not even the candidates.

This omission should now be corrected. Electors should be allowed to decline the offer of being represented or governed by anyone at all. They may be foolish to do so but it is a legitimate choice.

The American people exercised it in the 1920s when they elected Calvin Coolidge to the White House, under the slogan 'Keep Cool With Coolidge'. By philosophy and temperament opposed to government, he spent more hours asleep than any other president. When Dorothy Parker heard the news of his death, she remarked, famously, "How could they tell?"

Electing someone like Coolidge is one way of voting against government, but it is arguably unfair on the Stay-At-Home party. It forces them to get out and vote *for* somebody and then to pay him a salary for doing nothing.

A simple alternative would be a law that no one is elected to any office, local or national, if voter turnout fell below a certain figure — say 20 per cent.

However, a superior proposal, which opens new democratic possibilities, would be to allow negative voting.

This system would give electors, as an alternative to voting for any candidate, the option of casting one vote against the candidate of their choice. This would give voters a valid way of saying "Anyone but that smarmy little toe-rag!" without spoiling their ballot papers.

For ease of counting, negative votes would be cast on differently coloured paper. They would be recorded as a minus vote against the relevant candidate, and the winner of any election would be decided on 'goal difference' — votes for minus those against.

Under this system it is quite possible that no candidate would have a positive goal difference. In that case nobody would be elected, and any salary, allowances and expenses would be saved until the next election.

Critics of negative voting will argue that it gives too much power to the cynical and the disenchanted. In fact, its effect would be quite the opposite. Since no one would get elected without a 'positive majority' it would force all candidates to think of good reasons for voting for them, instead of slinging mud at their opponents.

Would not that be a refreshing change?

Why Can't The English?...

THE CITY of Carlisle saw a landmark victory for free speech.

A local plasterer won a case for unfair dismissal against an employer who sacked him for refusing to sign a no-swearing agreement.

If the decision had gone the other way, the courts might have had to rule on what makes a swear word. They would have to take account of changing fashions. 'Golly!' and 'Gosh!' — which are safe enough in the pages of Enid Blyton — were once appalling variations on the name of God.

But the courts have been making case law since the twelfth century, when Henry I imposed savage punishments for swearing within a royal palace — a 40-shilling fine for a duke, forty pence for a yeoman and a whipping for a page. Swear-words then were almost all religious in origin: they made casual references to God, or Jesus Christ, or the saints. By Chaucer's time, three centuries later, a more secular Britain had added sex, excretion, xenophobia and class to the sources of swearing.

"You blackguard!" — a fierce mediaeval insult — originally meant "you cleaner of pots and pans!"

People swear for two reasons: either to release immediate emotions (as when a hammer comes into contact with a thumb) or to insult someone else.

In both cases, conventional swear-words are losing their power. Our society has become so tolerant of them in speech and print that they no longer wound or shock — although it is depressing to hear them so frequently from children. For Billy Bunter and his chums, it was a deadly insult to call someone a cad, or a bounder or even a frabjous ass.

The Remove today, even their five-year-old brothers and

sisters, routinely use language that would make a sailor blush.·

For their sake, we should encourage imaginative alternatives to swearing. The late great WC Fields managed to put a wealth of invective into the blameless expressions "Drat!", "Godfrey Daniel!" and "Mother of pearl!"

For insults, Shakespeare provides a treasure trove without resorting to four-letter words. In King Lear, Kent berates Oswald as "thou whoreson zed! thou unnecessary letter!" Margaret of Anjou lets fly at Richard III as a 'cacodemon', an 'elvish-marked, abortive rooting hog' and a 'slander of thy mother's heavy womb!'

Any of these would form a rich and satisfying way to curse the **** who pinches your parking place.

Better still, we should replenish our stockpile of abuse from another language.

I recommend Yiddish. There is no richer vocabulary of insult, and none which offers so many fine gradations.

It has a particularly useful range of words to describe a mediocrity or a nonentity or a bore — such as *nebbish,* or *nudnik* or *shlemiel.* A particularly sad version could be a *shnook* and a desperately stupid one might be a *golem.* Someone who combines mediocrity with the ability to talk baloney for hours on end might be a *fonfer.*

These words would be ideally suited to everyday use. They could be applied readily to a dreary colleague at your place of work, or those Awful Other People in your holiday resort.

But they would come into their own in the forthcoming General Election — as a perfect description of your least favourite politician. Try rehearsing it now.

"That (insert chosen name) is a complete fonfer!" Don't you feel better already?

***

FOR some time in the United States it has been a reckless, indeed almost criminal, act to use unflattering language about a woman, a member of an ethnic minority, a homosexual man or woman, a fat, short or stupid person, or another animal species (including a fish insect crustacean or mollusc).

Now at last the Americans have decided to protect one of the saddest victims of prejudice and incorrectness.

They have made it an offence to insult a vegetable.

A number of enlightened states have passed Agricultural Disparagement laws. They happen to be states with a big farm lobby, but it would be wrong to question their motives.

Fruit and vegetables have had a raw deal from society. They deserve respect and protection.

The new laws threaten with punitive damages anyone who makes an uncomplimentary remark about an agricultural product if it cannot be supported by scientific data.

There is a legendary New Yorker cartoon of a little girl confronting a plate of broccoli and saying "I say it's spinach, and I say the hell with it!" That little madam could now end up in court, wishing she'd put her greens in her mouth and shut it.

Fruit and vegetables have endured centuries of prejudice in language. "He's a vegetable... a cabbage... a total prune... that car is a complete lemon." All these are a disgraceful way to describe our botanical companions. And why should the Americans be allowed to use "he's a fruit" to describe an effeminate man?

I have seen fruit in every part of the United States — apples, pears, grapes, oranges, blueberries, bananas, even twists of lime — and never seen any of them camp around in sequinned dresses or even wear discreet make-up.

On the rare occasions when fruit and vegetables are used as a compliment the context is invariably sexist or discriminatory. "She's a hot tomato... she's a peach... come to me, my sweet potato..." Have these terms ever been applied to a man? In Carry-On films does any part of the *male* anatomy get referred to as 'a lovely pear'?

Why should only cucumbers win compliments for being cool? There's many an unsung swede that's shown steady nerves in a crisis. And I have never heard any fine words applied to a parsnip, even a buttered one.

Modern poets and songwriters have turned their backs on fruit and veg. Why couldn't Frank Sinatra sing "Courgettes,

I've had a few, but then again, too few to mention?" And it would have been just as good a climax to say "But more, much more than this, I did eat marrow."

The new American laws have their part to play but it will take many years before Western society conquers its cultural prejudice against fruit and vegetables. But things are slowly getting better.

I discovered this at a crowded publishing party to launch a new novel about a heartwarming romance between a tomato and an aubergine (it was called Le Rouge Et Le Noir).

"There's a terrific squash in here," said the author.

In a flash I replied "And there's a turnip for the book."

***

ESSEX Man has conquered France. There are now more Kevins in Paris than there are in Plaistow (and Chigwell, and Brentwood, and Ongar and Billericay and even Harlow).

From nowhere, Kevin has become the most popular boy's name in France. We may associate it with footballers (and football supporters), and Maxwell brothers, and cars with His and Her names in the front window. But the French find it sophisticated, elegant, and très snob. One little French boy in thirty has been called Kevin in the last five years — and they even pronounce it our way, without trying to Gallicize it into K'van.

To many French diehards the infant Kevins are another symptom of the collapse of French culture against its Anglo-Saxon invaders, just as le café is giving way to le snack-bar. But that theory holds no water: Kevin is not an Anglo-Saxon name but Irish and Gaelic (meaning handsome). If the French had wanted to call their boys handsome they would have called them Beau, like dozens of fine Southern gentlemen in the United States.

Others put the blame on Kevin Costner, but this too is silly: the French have enough wooden actors of their own.

Whatever their reason for acquiring the name, the new

French generation can take inspiration from some great Kevins of the past.

My saint's directory identifies St Kevin as a sixth-century Irish nobleman who founded a monastic community. According to legend, be lived to be 120, on a diet of salmon brought to him by a trained otter. This is wildly implausible, since no otter could live to be 120.

An alternative is St Kevin of Cortina, patron (in company with St Tracey) of reformed gamblers, identified by their symbol of giant cuddly dice.

In both Britain and the United States Kevins had their boom years in the 1960s. It entered the British name charts quietly in 1921 but was extremely rare before the war. By 1950 it had gained ground: from a sample of 10,000 newborn boys in that year, ninety eight were Kevins. By 1960 that proportion had risen to 279 and in 1965 it was holding its own at 254. The 1970s and 1980s saw a slump and by 1990 there were only twenty six mewling and puking Kevins in the sample 10,000 — they had even fallen behind the Kierans.

In the United States, Kevin appeared out of nowhere in 1960 in eleventh place among boys' names — ahead of Richard, for goodness sake. It was but a passing fad. By 1970 it had fallen out of the top fifty (while Richard held on to number 19). But by 1993 it was back again: in 29th place for white boys and 15th for non-whites, with Richard well down the field. I blame the little brat in Home Alone (and I was always on the side of the burglars).

Time alone will tell whether the French continue to shop for their boys' names on our side of the Channel.

Their current runners-up to Kevin are mostly traditional French: Alexandre, Maxime, and Nicolas. But I am intrigued by another new entry in the French top five. Jordan. Jordan has a very Kevin quality about it. The two could easily be brothers.

Watch out for the two French presidential contenders in the year 2051. If they are called Wayne Jospin and Darren Chirac — and if Kevin Köhl is the first to congratulate the winner — united Europe will at last look like a possibility.

***

AS A playwright, Sarah Mason may or may not have what it takes to win an audience but she certainly knows how to wow an advertiser.

She managed to persuade makers of crisps, bras and fortified wine to pay up to £1600 for a mention of their brands in her play Skin, on its tour of the south of England.

Ms Mason is by no means the first dramatist to display such commercial acumen.

For many years scholars have wondered how Shakespeare managed to get rich and change his social status from tradesman's son to man of property. It was certainly not from writing and acting, which were low-life and low-paid occupations. There is now a wild theory that he supplemented his income by spying.

Wrong. The newly discovered 'Hyper' Quarto has revealed that Shakespeare too was a master of product placement. It enables us at last to enjoy the text of his plays as it was actually heard by his target audiences.

Take, for example, Macb..., sorry, The Scottish play. The Quarto shows that the famous sleepwalking scene should be played as follows.

> Lady M: Out, damned spot! out I say! Jif Microliquid, where art thou?
>
> Enter a small bottle.
>
> Bottle: Here madam. But not all my micropower can pluck from memory a rooted sorrow Nor raze the written troubles of the mind.

The opening lines of Richard III should read:

> "Now is the winter of our discontent
> But Lunn-Poly holidays are down ten per cent."

Hamlet's tortured musings originally had a much sharper focus. "Whatever you want to be or not to be you'll be or not be it better with Prudential." The same company can also now be recognized as the sponsor of the "seven pension ages of man" in As You Like It.

The character of Henry V has long been an enigma. What makes him change so suddenly from a boozy delinquent to a straight-laced warrior? The mystery is cleared by the Quarto's revelation of the hitherto missing scene in which Prince Hal stops drinking sack with Falstaff and orders instead his first pint of Heineken.

The infant TSB used Shakespeare's talents well in A Midsummer Night's Dream: "I know a bank whereon the wild thyme blows Whose managers say Ayes and never Noes." An early form of the credit card was promoted in Richard II: "all places that the eye of heaven visits Are to a Visa man ports and happy havens."

Always short of money, Shakespeare was forced to take his advertising commitments very seriously indeed. We can see this when Hamlet upbraids two players for over-acting in endorsements for a denture cleaner and a department store: "I would have such a fellow whipp'd for o'erdoing Steradent; it out-harrods Harrods."

But Shakespeare revealed his true feelings towards his commercial writing in one of his comedies. The title has been garbled through the years but the new 'Hyper' Quarto again reveals Shakespeare's true version: Ads Do Much About Nothing.

The play's real hero, Dogberry, delivers this commentary on the advertising men with whom Shakespeare stooped to conquer the Elizabethan consumer: "Marry sir, they have committed false report; moreover, they have spoken untruths; secondarily, they are slanders; sixth and lastly they have belied an ad daily; thirdly they have verified unjust things; and to conclude, they are lying knaves."

***

THE LAST bastion has fallen, and the barbarians are inside the citadel of the English language.

The new Chambers 21st Century Dictionary says that it is quite permissible to split an infinitive.

When I was taught English it was easier to split the atom than an infinitive, and quite right too. The two words of an infinitive, such as 'to love and to cherish' or 'to have and to hold', should cleave together like newly-weds: no man should put them asunder with an adverb.

I blame Star Trek, which produced the most famously split infinitive in the world. Captain Kirk promised 'to boldly go'. He could just as easily have promised 'to go boldly', and he would have added a touch of poetry by inversion: 'boldly to go where none have gone before'.

Such is the natural aversion to the split infinitive that the listener's first reaction is to assume that the captain has invented a brand-new verb 'to boldligo'. As such, the word has a Latin American ring: 'it takes two to boldligo'.

Split infinitives are like split ends, messy and distressing but easily avoidable with a little verbal conditioning. Sometimes the split infinitive offers a tempting pathway to clarity, as in "I fail completely to understand you." This suggests that the speaker understands nothing at all, as would moving 'completely' to the end of the sentence.

But suppose the speaker wanted to suggest partial understanding. He might easily be lured into "I fail to completely understand you." But it would be easier still to avoid the infinitive altogether: "I do not fully understand you."

The new dictionary threatens to cause further outrage by permitting the use of 'infer' to mean the same thing as 'imply'. It passes an implied (or inferred) judgment on possible objectors, by advising readers to avoid such usage in communicating "to someone who is likely to be precise about language."

You can almost feel the pity in those words: you can almost hear the words 'crank, pedant, fussbudget'. If you ask for good English, people will think you are Victor Meldrew.

It is, incidentally, a powerful comment on modern society that the word 'purist' has become a term of abuse.

English is a living language; with over 400 million speakers it is second only to Mandarin. Its usages can never be frozen; people will speak and write English like what they choose, and if enough of them decide to change current usage they will prevail over academies and lexicographers.

But those who set up as guardians of the language should still prefer euphony to ugliness, precision to muddle, discipline to sloppiness. They should teach young people that grammar is not just someone who is married to Grandpa.

Good English is an act of courtesy to a reader or listener: it shows a willingness to take trouble and minimize the task of understanding. It shows the same courtesy as speaking clearly in preference to mumbling (and you cannot get a consonant these days from anyone under thirty).

Good English is also one of the pillars of our liberties. When words are allowed to mean anything at all, it is easier for those in power to lie to us.

Thanks For The Memory

THE COFFEE stain on my tie is the size of the Atlantic Ocean. The red spot on my nose is as big as the planet Jupiter's. And as for my mind — that is the biggest Black Hole in the Universe...

I am just seconds away from my first appearance as a contestant on Mastermind, and I cannot remember anything at all. When Magnus Magnusson asks me my name I will say 'Pass'. Occupation? After the next two minutes it will be '*Former* journalist'. Special subject? Humiliation.

For nearly twenty five years, some twelve hundred contestants have asked themselves the same question on their way to that terrible black chair: why did I let myself in for this?

It all began in an Indian Railway carriage on the way to Jaipur, eighteen months ago. I was on a cricket tour of India with the Fleet Street journalists XI. To pass the time on a slow journey with no buffet car, we divided ourselves into four teams and set ourselves a long series of general knowledge quizzes. I found that I knew just about all the answers. And it was not just a fluke, because I found that the same thing happened on the way to Madras, Bangalore and Bombay. I was disqualified from any of the teams and asked instead to set the grand final quiz for our farewell dinner.

At that dinner, fatally weakened by Kingfisher beer and local whisky, I heard the fatal words "You'll have to go in for Mastermind." When I demurred, I was told that the full horror-story of a certain missed catch on the boundary at Madras would be revealed to the British public.

I had it coming to me. I have always been able to remember useless information. I can tell anyone the date of the Peace of Westphalia (1648), but not the PIN number of my cashcard. I can find Alma-Ata on a map of the world, but not my house keys on the mantlepiece.

My application (by postcard) to be a contestant was answered by a polite letter and a form asking me to name not just one but three special subjects. (It takes three to get to the final, and now they all have to be different.)

The form also asked for basic personal details and 'any interesting information about yourself'. This is arguably the toughest question you get asked on Mastermind. Should I mention my refusal of last year's Nobel Prize for Literature? No, don't invent. When in doubt, tell the truth...

Choosing a special subject took a lot of care. I knew that if I did become a contestant it could easily take over my life. I might have to read about it for weeks on end. I wanted something or someone I really liked — with some light relief.

That is why for my first special subject I chose Harry Truman, the dapper, resolute, Give-Em-Hell postwar President of the United States. He took huge decisions which shaped the modern world — without ever once consulting an opinion pollster or a spin doctor. His Presidency was not only full of history it was full of colour. At the height of the Korean war, he found time to threaten to kick a music critic for a lukewarm review of his daughter's singing.

Second subject (if required) would also be history: British politics between the wars. For third subject, a complete change: the career of Sir Garfield Sobers.

Mastermind rejects special subjects for being arcane (Roads To And From Letchworth) or for being done too often. Would mine fail at this first hurdle? Harry and Garry did the trick. I was invited to an audition. It consisted primarily of a general knowledge test. The questions were noticeably tougher than those of the programme ("Which Shakespearean character was a 'snapper up of unconsidered trifles'?") But there was no camera and no time limit. The production team simply wanted some idea of how much I knew. Then some more personal questions and general conversation, to test whether I might fluff or faint in front of the camera.

Some weeks later the fatal letter arrived. I was to be a contestant. My first round would be some ten weeks away — in the historic, ornate Drapers Hall in the City of London. Would I arrive there in mid-afternoon for an evening recording? Would I be sure not to wear camera-dazzling clothes or a T-shirt with an advertising slogan? Meanwhile would I give them a reading list of books on Harry S Truman, which would be used by an outside expert to set the questions?

I gave them a list. It included a 1500-page biography — if I was going to swot, they could damn well swot too...

For the next ten weeks, I lived in a time-warp with Harry Truman. No event interested me unless it happened between 1945 and 1953. I read and read about him and took 10,000 words of notes, first in longhand and then transcribed onto the word processor. All my study came from books. I tried once to study him through the Internet: I found it useless, a jumble of unco-ordinated references.

For Christmas, among other gifts my partner gave me a teddy bear with a combative expression and a paw chopping the air — as Truman did when giving a speech. We named him Harry.

I had resolved initially not to try to revise general knowledge. Either I would know it or not. But this resolve soon collapsed into panic. I dived randomly into reference books and tried to remember huge lists of operas, Greek myths, capital cities and scientific laws. By far the best source was a picture encyclopedia belonging to my partner's eight-year-old son.

I ploughed remorselessly through Harry Truman. A few nights before the contest I had a vivid dream that I was a member of his Cabinet during the Korean war. I was pleased, but I wondered how much use the subconscious would be on Mastermind.

The day itself began with a piece of low farce.

In best suit and tie, but with a persistent red spot on my nose, I set off for the Drapers' Hall in the City of London for the recording. And I could not find the entrance. I walked around for nearly an hour, envisaging a newspaper headline: 'MASTERMIND CONTESTANT LOST IN CITY. Memory man cannot find historic Livery Hall.'

Finally the sight of a BBC broadcast van gave me a clue.

Fortunately, being a neurotic about keeping appointments, I had given myself over an hour to spare.

I met the other three contestants. They were not rivals, but fellow-victims: Nicholas Henley, factory worker, doing the history of artillery, Patricia Gould, retired teacher doing Charles I, and Sally Budd, secretary and partner in her husband's photographic business, doing Vivien Leigh. None of us could believe what we were doing.

Two rounds were being recorded back-to-back, and all eight contestants had a briefing with Magnus Magnusson and the producer, David Mitchell. The other contest included a close-cropped woman with the adopted name Viv Acious, doing Aphra Benn. She refused to disclose her given name. A witty-looking young man named Boris Starling, a political risk consultant, was offering the adventures of Tintin.

We were reminded of the rules and advised to guess an answer rather than pass. Magnus took great care to settle his descriptions of us — and even more in trying to put us all at ease. In spite of his genuine empathy, I still dribbled BBC coffee onto my tie.

We did a rehearsal (general knowledge only) which gave our first experience of The Chair. Physically, it was very comfortable — but I could not wait to get out of it, and tried to bolt too early when the test questions were over. "Wait a moment, Mr Heller," said Magnus kindly but firmly, "I have not thanked you yet."

The ornate Hall was full of Royal portraits, including Lawrence s George IV. I did some on-the-spot revision, reigns, dates, consorts, principal events...

The make-up lady toned down my nasal spot, and a re-knotted tie concealed the worst of the coffee. But then came a long wait. I paced, I tranced, I made many visits to the cloak-room.

Once I caught a glimpse of Magnus's private preparations. It is bad enough preparing one special subject, but in effect he has to master four with every programme — never fluffing a proper name, never accepting an incorrect answer, never allowed to pass...

As the minutes ticked by, I could feel my memory start to

implode. Who was this Harry S Truman? I found myself remembering more about Vivien Leigh. Well, fiddle-de-dee...

I had resolved not to read my notes, but suddenly I desperately needed the name of the White House secretary in the mink coat (who figured in a minor scandal of the Truman years). I could not believe that it would be asked but I just had to know it. Riffle-riffle through the pages. Of course, it was Mrs Young.

My spectators arrived. Yes, I told my partner, I am wearing her lucky Maori charm. Thank you all so much for coming to support, but now would you please go away — to a country where this programme is not shown? I spotted Peter Bottomley MP. Why? At least he proved a distraction.

To make matters worse, my contest was the second to be recorded and we were led in to watch the first.

Their general knowledge questions seemed fiendish. I could hardly answer one. The record low score on Mastermind was 12. I felt sure I was going to break it. Should I faint — or make a dash for the Swiss border?

Too late. The first contest ended (Boris Starling victorious) and the BBC guards closed around us. They took us back to the waiting room. Some late powdering and tidying and then we were marched to the set. The familiar execution music came up (Yah-ta-ta-tah. *Daah-dah.*)

Soon it was time for the loneliest journey in television. The Chair no longer seemed comfortable but cavernous. The Black Out.

With a mighty effort of memory I got through name, occupation and special subject. Then came Magnus's familiar intonation "... starting Now."

First ball of the innings: "who was the Chief Justice who swore in Harry Truman as President of the United States?"

It hit the middle of the bat. At least it would not be a duck...

Quite suddenly, all of Harry Truman came back to me. I leant forward in The Chair, almost as if to breathe the questions. There was only one I did not know, and I made a very good guess at it. Mrs Young did not appear.

Nineteen at the half-way stage and a lead of four. Before general knowledge a longer introduction from Magnus. To my delight he read out the full title of my book, and quite slowly: "A-Tale-Of-Ten-Wickets". It was all I could do not to bawl out "Published by Oval Publishing at £5.99!"

No alarms in general knowledge. One pass over a fierce mathematics question. My lead increased and I could sense a runaway win. But my nerves were still with me and by gum! I tried once again to leave The Chair too early.

Handshakes. Euphoria. My spectators ecstatic. Schmoozing and decompression in the post-contest reception. Magnus was particularly nice to my invitees. How many Mastermind receptions has he done — over six hundred? — but he has remembered that this one, like the previous 599, was special and unique to other people...

Still euphoric when I returned home, I also felt sad to say goodbye to Harry S Truman, a friend, a part of my life.

I sat in a chair for a long time and did something very strange. I read a book for pleasure.

(*Extended version of piece published in The Mail On Sunday*)

Also by RICHARD HELLER
A TALE OF TEN WICKETS

His first novel—a Canterbury Tales for village cricket—weaves into a thrilling match the secret lives of the visiting players.

"This delightful tome resonates with barely suppressed English passion for the sport of flannelled fools. He manages to cram the outlines of ten novels into a paperback about one village game."

Peter McKay: The Daily Mail

"Some of the stories are beauties, vignettes of triumph and disaster in which the characters are illuminated with real sharpness."

Max Davidson: The Daily Telegraph

"Amateurs of all ages will feel at home in the bucolic atmosphere on pitch and in pavilion."

Duff Hart-Davis: The Mail On Sunday

"A book full of cricket and wit, told with a true passion for the game."

Kate Hoey MP: The Evening Standard

Paperback original by Oval Publishing £5.99

To order a signed copy, please complete the form below

To Department M, Oval Publishing
30 Crewdson Road, London SW9 0LJ
tel and fax 0171 582 4892

From: (name) ————————————————

(address) ————————————————

Please supply ——— copies of A Tale Of Ten Wickets at £6-50 each.
I enclose a cheque/PO for £ ——— payable to 'Oval Publishing'.

Please inscribe book(s) to ————————————